LeRoy Neiman

ART &
LIFE STYLE

LeRoy Neiman

ART & LIFE STYLE

FELICIE - PUBLISHERS - NEW YORK

Design: Edvins Strautmanis
Editorial consultant: Mickey Herskowitz

The works appearing on pages 23, 32, 38, 47, 48, 59, 60, 64,
66, 69, 70, 75, 133, 190, 193, copyright © *Playboy*
Library of Congress catalog card number: 74-8355
ISBN 0-9600-692-3-2
First printing
Printed and bound in Italy

For Janet

FELICIE · PUBLISHERS · NEW YORK

CONTENTS

INTRODUCTION

A day at the races,
A night at the opera...

These two lines, I think, reflect the spirit of my work and my pleasures, my art and my life style. In a sense they capture the range of my environment. I have painted and sketched in casinos, hotels, bars, massage parlors, steam baths, in the salons of elegant restaurants (and sometimes their galleys), on battlefields and football fields, in law courts and tennis courts, in pool rooms and swimming pools, from the decks of luxury liners and yachts and the doorways of skid-row missions. To me it's all Neimanland.

Through all these tableaux I have marched to my own drummer, as conscious of stable boys and dishwashers as I am of the wealthy horseman and the imperious maître d' and his compatriot diner.

There are times when art functions best at a level of the commonplace. Mine goes to the people. My art is there, for the people—the artist surrounded by the truth in which he grew and lives. The artist paints his own range of feelings about a situation—not a facsimile but the moving spirit of a scene, creating his own environment.

We applaud the sensitive hands of the painter, the pianist, the conductor, the quarterback, the croupier—but the hands of the tradesman, the farmer, the carpenter, the electrician and the plumber lend their strength to our daily lives. I once traded a painting to a plumber in return for a sink that he installed in my studio. Fair exchange, my art for his. Janet was once given a Balenciaga suit by a grand down-and-out countess in Paris for a portrait I had done of her when she couldn't meet my fee.

9

Epron '66
LeRoy Neiman

The human being is affected by the mood and performance of other people. He must take their activities into account. Each organism lives in and by means of its environment. Man is constantly trying to achieve a more satisfying adjustment with his environment, seeking to control it by a continuing interplay of internal processes with external conditions or events. A group gambling at a roulette table is a perfect example and one of my favorite subjects.

Professional sports I regard as entertainment and amusement, where spectators and business are equally important. For the athlete, what was fun as a kid becomes business as a pro. But still, deep down, the paying spectator never has the fun of involvement the paid athlete has. It is more fun to do something well than to watch something well done. If painting wasn't fun for me I wouldn't do it. This is at the heart of what my work is about.

For me and for most of us, the army and religion, at certain impressionable times in life, are more or less compulsory. Religion appeals to a man's spirit; the military to his sense of duty. You can't escape their influence, once recruited.

In the military service I often related the enlisted man to the officer, as later I related the artist to the officialdom of art. A man's time in the army is a touchstone for all his years — just as the man who has served time relates to prison the rest of his life. Both have been stamped by discipline.

If nothing else, the army completely confirmed me as an artist. During this period I made my crucial discovery of the difference between the life styles of the officer and the PFC. This was to become the basis for my later mission in art, to investigate life's social strata from the workingman to the multimillionaire. I discovered that while the poor I knew so well are so often pitiable, the rich can be fools.

As an army cook I achieved my introductory education as an artist. I often painted murals in the army kitchens in which I performed my culinary wonders. In addition, I painted flattering officer portraits and in return was spared certain bothersome duties. My talents were also drafted to meet a growing market for VD posters. The army somehow managed to give its troops the impression that they had nothing to fear but venereal disease. These posters represented some of my better early work—it bordered on pornography. So one can see my early experiences as an artist were functional and practical. An early training for what would become my *modus operandi* as an artist.

This self-designed art apprenticeship in the army, together with the GI Bill funding of my formal art schooling, total up to a very positive assist from the military.

Four sound prerequisites for the artist's motivation also aided me from the outset: 1) He should begin life at the poverty level; 2) come from a broken home; 3) be a high school dropout; and 4) have an undistinguished military career.

I had another early advantage. My mother had the foresight to endow me with a black first name and a Jewish surname. People tend to assume that I possess both soul and financial acumen.

Whether sketching in the dark in the early days at strip joints (until a goon would heave me out), or later fraternizing with the clubhouse set at the racetrack, or mingling in the world of cabaret and casinos, the same cast would always hold forth; like a troupe they traveled ensemble from season to season, around the clock. My scenes are punctuated with recurring figures such as the gambler, the black man and the socialite.

westchester '70

Santa Anita LeRoy Neiman '64

Marigold Garden Chicago 1960 LeRoy Neiman

For example, I position the colorful gambler as a hoodlum type standing in the doorway of a desolate late-hour girlie club where he could be manager, bouncer or lookout. He turns up again, hanging around the gyms in my paintings of fighters at training. He is seen lurking about at the weigh-in the day of a big fight, or at the dog tracks of Miami Beach or Dublin. He's at Manhattan massage parlors, at Freeport crap tables. He sits in on all-night poker games, he favors fat Havana cigars and doesn't shave until dusk.

Then there is the reliable black. He is the groom leading the thoroughbred; the corner man carrying the pail down the aisle to the ring at the fights; the caddy toting bags at a golf classic. He is also the baggage handler at air terminals and train stations; or selling out Carnegie Hall with his music; or bringing 90,000 fans to their feet at the Super Bowl with a long run. Always, as he does his number, he handles himself smartly and with dignity—ever the indispensable pro. I'm always armed with felt-nib pens filled with sepia ink for drawing black people, because every important sporting or social scene has its percentage of blacks—either performing service chores or having been admitted to the competitive struggle of the social select.

The same lady socialite can turn up dining at a grand restaurant, at a chemin de fer table, at a cocktail party or bar, in the paddock and clubhouse box at the races, first row ringside at the fights, in the dress circle at the opera, or having her Vuitton luggage and her Halston body searched at customs.

A veteran bartender at the Polo Lounge in the Beverly Hills Hotel back in 1957 once told me he had seen two bar paintings of mine on exhibit in Los Angeles, and the paintings, he said, had given him a whole new feeling about the back bar, the duckboards, the light hitting the bottles, the labels,

the haze of smoke in the room, even the cash registers. It made tending bar a whole new aesthetic experience. He had discovered beauty where before he had found none. And this was in the pre-pop art days.

When I paint, I seriously weigh the public presence of a person—the surface façade. I am less concerned with how people look when they wake up or how they act at home. A person's public presence reflects his own efforts at image development. When a man reaches success his weight will change—if fat he'll get fatter or thinner; if thin he'll get bonier or fatter. Salvador Dali pulls long hairs from his head and waxes them into his fabulous moustache. Once, when we were posing for a photograph together, the cameraman suggested I do away with my favorite accessory—the cigar. Ever prop-conscious, Dali insisted, "Keep it. It is good for the photo."

Vanities are always up front—the appareled body is important. The hairstyle, maquillage, other cosmetic details or decorations such as moustaches, beards, muttonchops and applied art—like hairpieces.

I am never fascinated enough to draw something, or someone, I find grotesque. I am drawn to affectations—say, a dude who puts his hat on backward—only if it creates an effect that enhances him to himself.

In the years that have passed since I painted the first of the works that appear in this book, vast and dramatic changes have taken place all around me. The most important single development has been the growth of television. It has been a dynamic force in my own success as an artist. Television has the capacity to deliver a drawing or a painting to an audience that, at any moment, might number 50 or more millions of people. It is immediate. It is intimate. Television adds another dimension: the opportunity for me to comment, on camera, over my work. It is magic. Pictures with words. The tube gives incredible fidelity to every color, tone, line, texture, even thumbprints. Television came along to circulate me and my work to more people than the Old Masters knew existed.

My preoccupation with "Man at his Leisure" naturally introduced me to major sports events, a hard world from which to escape. As time passes, you find that you do not

In Paris in 1971, Neiman discusses etchings with Dunoyer de Segonzac, who has worked over 7,600 copper plates. Posing with Salvador Dali in New York, 1972. In 1973, Muhammad Ali looks over Neiman's shoulder as he sketches.

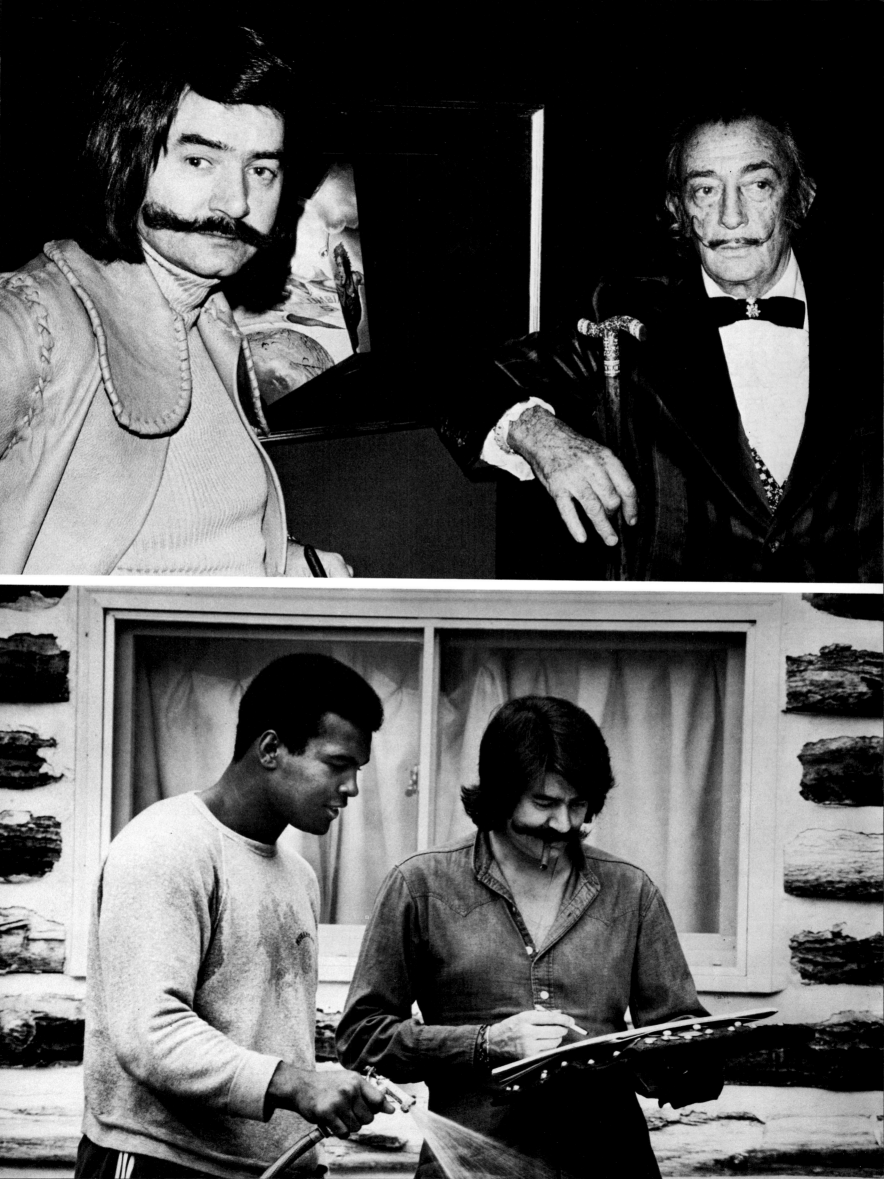

namath '68

wish to escape at all. Sports and television formed a perfect marriage in the 1960s, one that led logically, for me, to the ultimate visual use—art on television. It is quite a triple play: on the spot from the artist's eye, through the camera's eye, to the public eye. Because the viewer has direct focus on a framed area, my art flashes on the screen with sock—instantaneously. A reportage sketch comes across with extra clout.

As a painter I am drawn to sports as a bird to the sky. It is all color and movement, a world of numbers, flags and geometric surfaces. It is a universe of green, from the gaming tables to the gridiron.

Much of my life has been spent involved with and observing people at play. It is a pleasant world to inhabit. The people in sport—and by that I mean those involved in leisure, as well as games—reflect the times and society, and they perform in the open, where we can judge their errors and weaknesses. They are people who have no secrets.

In life, as in art, I have always subscribed to a quote in a Stendhal tale about lovers: "Believe what you see rather than what you are told."

PAINTINGS
AND DRAWINGS

AUX DEUX MAGOTS 1961
oil, 49" x 72¼"
Collection of Mr. Harrison Eiteljorg, Indianapolis, Indiana

GREEN TABLE 1972 ▶
oil, 72" x 48"
Collection of the artist

ALABAMA HAND-OFF 1973
oil, 31" x 44"
Collection of Mr. Mayer Mitchell, Mobile, Alabama

LABOR AND MANAGEMENT 1966 ▶
oil, 24" x 17¼"
Mr. and Mrs. Erwin Weiner, Chicago, Illinois

PREMIERE, METROPOLITAN OPERA 1966
oil, 44" x 54½"
Collection of Mrs. E. A. Coleman, Fort Lauderdale, Florida

22

SURFING AT HUNTINGTON BEACH 1966
oil, 42" x 60"
From the Playboy Collection

(next page)
ALI-FRAZIER FIGHT 1971 ▶
oil, 48" x 72"
Collection of the artist

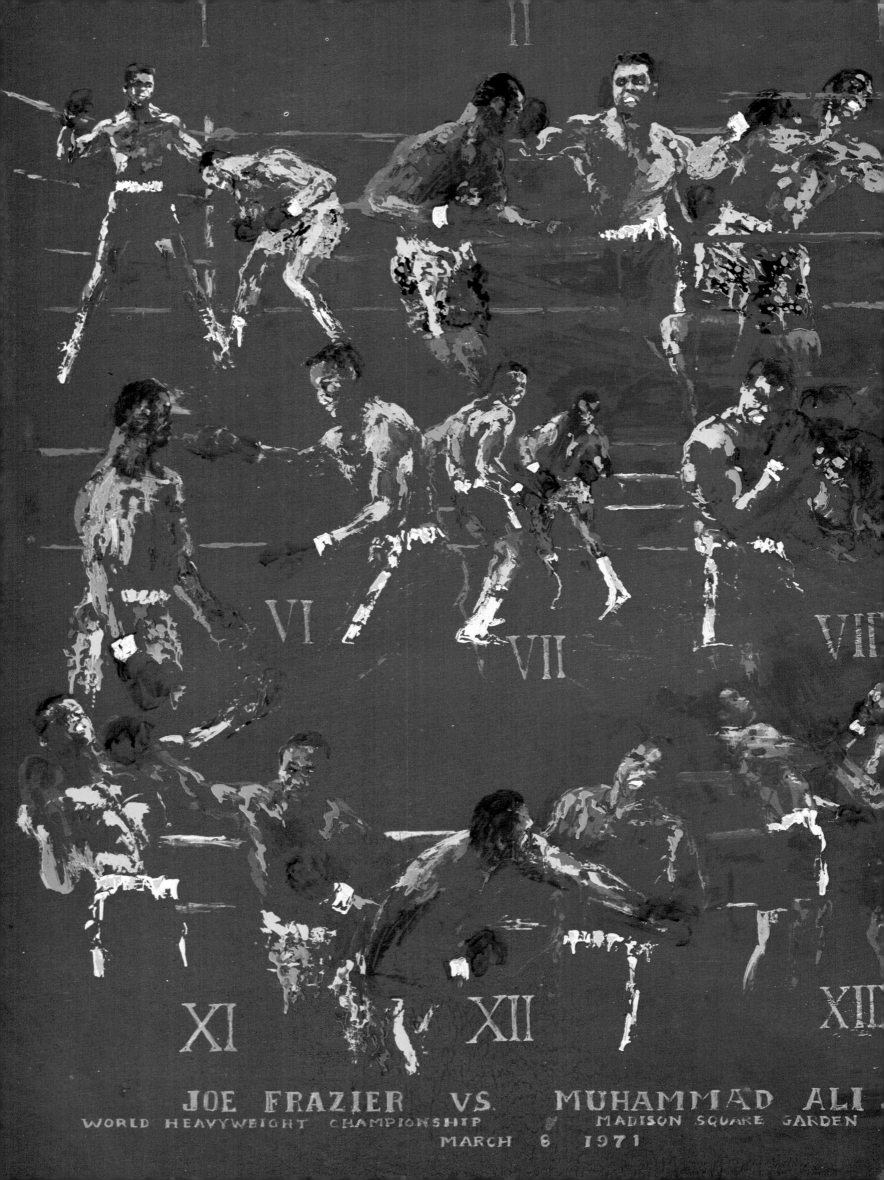

JOE FRAZIER VS. MUHAMMAD ALI
WORLD HEAVYWEIGHT CHAMPIONSHIP   MADISON SQUARE GARDEN
MARCH 8 1971

IX

X

IVX

XV

YORK

LeRoy Neiman '71

83313

PADDOCK LADIES 1973
oil, 23¾" x 17⅜"
Private collection, Chicago, Illinois

DETAIL OF PADDOCK LADIES ▶

MONTE CARLO HARBOUR 1960
oil, 48" x 72"
Collection of Mr. Carl-Wilhelm Busse, Bielefeld, West Germany

BLACK BREAK 1973 ▶
oil, 26" x 20"
Collection of the artist

SECRETARIAT STRUNG OUT 1973
oil, 20" x 24"
Collection of Mr. Peter D. Tattersall, Alexandria, Louisiana

THE GET SHOT 1973
silk-screen print, 12" x 28"
Edition of 300
Published by Felicie, Inc.

◀ **THE SLOPESTER 1969**
oil, 20" x 11¾"
Private collection, Cleveland, Ohio

NATIONAL HORSE SHOW 1967
oil on black paper, 24" x 30"
From the Playboy Collection

SINGLES 1971 ▶
oil, 48" x 36"
Collection of the artist

LeRoy Neiman '71

CLUB CHEZ REGINE 1961
oil, 50½" x 63⅛"
Collection of Mr. Harrison Eiteljorg, Indianapolis, Indiana

BENGAL TIGER 1971
oil, 48" x 36"
Collection of Mr. L. Roy Papp, Chicago, Illinois

GRAND FOYER, METROPOLITAN OPERA 1966–67
oil, 44" x 54½"
Collection of Mrs. E. A. Coleman, Fort Lauderdale, Florida

GRAND ESCALIER, PARIS OPERA 1969 ▶
oil, 54" x 44"
Collection of Mrs. E. A. Coleman, Fort Lauderdale, Florida

BACKSTAGE AT THE LIDO 1962
charcoal, 30" x 40"
From the Playboy Collection

38

TOURNAMENT GOLF 1973
silk-screen print, 22½″ x 32″
Edition of 300
Published by Felicie, Inc.

(next page)
INTRODUCTION AT MADISON SQUARE GARDEN 1964-65 ▶
oil, 72″ x 118″
Collection of Madison Square Garden Corporation, New York City

Madison Square Garden
LeRoy Neiman '4-65

SLAP SHOT 1969
oil on paper, 22" x 28⅝"
Collection of Mr. George Barr, Chicago, Illinois

COUNCIL OF WAR 1962 ▶
oil, 47½" x 28⅛"
Private collection, Chicago, Illinois

44

LION FAMILY PORTRAIT 1971
oil, 36" x 48"
Collection of Mrs. Amory L. Haskell, Jr., Palm Beach, Florida

◀SONNY LISTON 1964
oil, 24" x 12"
Collection of Mr. and Mrs. Frank Bond, Baltimore, Maryland

SATCHMO HEAD 1967
oil, 20¾" x 20¾"
Collection of Mr. and Mrs. Alvin Wolf, Coral Gables, Florida

LIDO 1963
oil, 24" x 48"
From the Playboy Collection

KATOUBIA PALACE, TANGIERS 1969 *(detail)*
oil, 29½" x 40¾"
Collection of Mrs. E. A. Coleman, Fort Lauderdale, Florida

ELMO'S 1965
oil, 14" x 16"
Collection of Mr. and Mrs. J. Russell Duncan, Palm Beach, Florida

◀ **POLO** 1964
oil, 72" x 48"
From the Playboy Collection

49

KIROV BALLET REHEARSAL 1969
oil, 54½" x 74
Collection of Dr. and Mrs. George Carter, New York City

ASCOT DOUBLE ENTRY 1969
oil, 22" x 18"
Mr. and Mrs. Erwin Weiner, Chicago, Illinois

JOCKEYS UP 1971
charcoal on paper, 44" x 76"
Collection of Mr. John W. Galbreath, Columbus, Ohio

THE KNOCKOUT 1967 ▶
oil, 31¼" x 23⅞"
Collection of Mr. and Mrs. Robert L. Wolfson, St. Louis, Missouri

SPECTATOR FLEET, AMERICA'S CUP 1964
oil, 48" x 72"
Collection of Mrs. E. A. Coleman, Fort Lauderdale, Florida

HARLEQUIN ON HORSEBACK 1971
oil, 52" x 48"
Collection of Mr. Roone Arledge, New York City

(next page)
PADDOCK PERSONALITIES 1972 ▶
charcoal on craft paper, 36" x 60"
Collection of Mr. and Mrs. Edward L. Bomze, New York City

MURRAY'S CABARET, LONDON 1966
oil, 48" x 72"
From the Playboy Collection

◄ BIRD AND DIZ 1973
  charcoal and varnish on craft paper, 40" x 29½"
  Collection of the artist

THE MIXOLOGIST 1957
oil, 48" x 72"
From the Playboy Collection

JOHN F. KENNEDY'S BIRTHDAY PARTY 1966 ▶
oil, 47½" x 43"
Collection of Madison Square Garden Corporation, New York City

President's Birthday Party
1962
Madison Square Garden
LeRoy Neiman 62

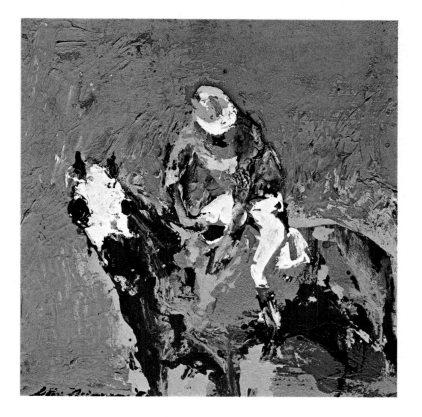

HORSE AND RIDER 1959
oil, 13" x 13"
Collection of Mr. and Mrs. Frank McMahon, Palm Beach, Florida

◄ **PANAMANIAN JOCKEY 1963**
oil, 9⅜" x 4¾"
Collection of Mr. Jack O'Brian, New York City

THE CUT MAN 1965
oil, 27¼" x 22⅞"
Collection of Mr. Allen Swift, New York City

LADIES OF THE HUNT 1959
charcoal on paper, 25½" x 38"
Collection of Mr. Victor Lownes, London

BAR REGULARS 1959
charcoal on paper, 36" x 108"
From the Playboy Collection

NAPOLEON AT WATERLOO 1968-71
oil, 72" x 90"
Collection of the artist

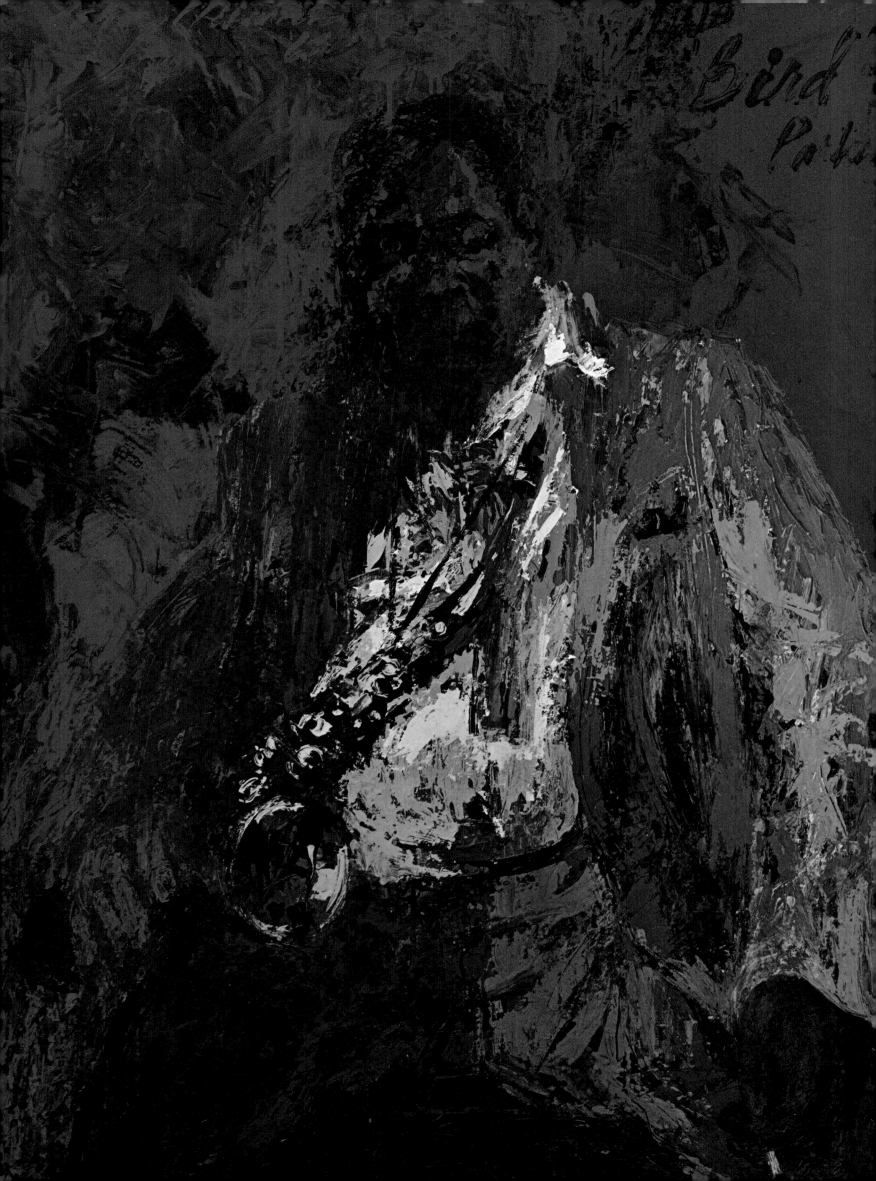

REGATTA OF THE GONDOLIERS 1969
oil, 29½" x 40½"
Collection of the artist

◀ CHARLIE "BIRD" PARKER 1964
oil, 48" x 36"
From the Playboy Collection

LEOPARD 1971
oil, 36" x 48"
Mr. and Mrs. Doyle W. Cotton, Jr., Aspen, Colorado

CIGARETTE GIRL 1959 ▶
oil, 96" x 48"
From the Playboy Collection

QUEEN'S JOCKEY AT EPSOM 1960
oil, 50" x 48"
From the Playboy Collection

CASINO AT MONTE CARLO 1969
oil, 48" x 60"
Collection of Mr. and Mrs. Robert L. Wolfson, St. Louis, Missouri

(next page)
MIDDLE AGE AT "21" 1973 ▶
oil, 48" x 72"
Collection of the artist

ON THE TURF 1966
oil, montage 23½" x 18"
Collection of Mr. and Mrs. Leonard Treister, Miami Beach, Florida

PUMP ROOM BAR 1956
oil, 48" x 72"
From the Playboy Collection

THE HUNT 1959
oil, 47½" x 71"
Collection of Mr. Shirley Percival, Jr., Des Moines, Iowa

RED SQUARE, MOSCOW 1969
oil, 48" x 60"
Collection of Mrs. E. A. Coleman, Fort Lauderdale, Florida

ASCOT PADDOCK 1960
oil, 52" x 59"
Private collection, St. Louis, Missouri

TOOTS SHOR'S BAR 1967–69
oil, 72" x 87"
Collection of Mr. and Mrs. Jack Wrather, Los Angeles, California

At Olympiastadion, München, 1972

HIS LIFE (and style)
—a chronology

Born June 8, 1927, in St. Paul, Minnesota....Father, Charley, roustabout, drifter, free spirit...in early years an auto racer of Barney Oldfield era....His uncle John, an immigrant, started as a horse trader, became the family legend as a Duluth millionaire contractor, building much of the Masabi Iron Range Railroad...later became a sportsman with a string of race horses....Mother, Lydia, thrice married, spirited and independent...father surpassed his mother's marital record by one for a combined total of seven, a prodigious feat for a couple not born to wealth or to Hollywood.

Education starts in parochial schools, streets and back alleys of St. Paul...as product of Depression, sandlot team sports and gang fighting compete for leisure time with ice skating and hockey...follows Bernie Bierman–style football, minor league baseball, ski jumping and motorcycle hill climbing...during state fair watches dirt-track auto racing and harness racing (no thoroughbred flat racing in St. Paul).

Church basement boxing is major recreation...sessions in the cellar of St. Vincent's Church are compulsory...John Dillinger is the neighborhood folk hero, an exciting figure compared to the unemployed fathers hanging around the house all day....A favorite amusement is to haunt locales where gangland shootings took place, sticking fingers in bullet holes.

In grade school, the only art practiced is the art of self-defense, as demonstrated by Mike Gibbons...boxing is popularized by a glut of boxing movies...all the leading stars of the day—Gable, Garfield, Cagney, Flynn—played prize-fight leads...in two decades more than 50 prize-fight films are produced, including *The Square Jungle, The Leather Pushers, The Set-Up, The Fighter, The Kid Comes Back, Iron Man, Right Cross, The Golden Gloves Story*...the movies of the day helped make boxing an obligation.

Despite lack of art environment, manages to put natural talent to use...tattoos schoolmates' arms during recess using regular pen and ink, resulting in many skin irritations and infections, as well as wrath of the good Sisters and parents...for years draws own comic strip at home...keeps it up daily, creating own characters and employing color on Sundays.

In sixth grade wins national art prize for painting of a swimming fish—which goes virtually unnoticed in family and school....From age 12 to 14 paints prices weekly on local grocery-store windows with colored calcimine, embellishing product names and prices with animated drawings of Thanksgiving turkeys, grazing cows, fruits, vegetables, porkers, catsup bottles, beer bottles and other art objects.

Frequently breaks away from street-corner buddies to study alone the gloomy portraits of governors in the Minnesota

Clark St. Chicago '55

State Capitol Building, fascinated by the technique with which glasses are painted on the subjects.

Every fall, works and travels with the Royal American Shows, Ripley's "Believe-it-or-not" Side Show...often called upon to use talent retouching huge canvas displayed in front of show depicting freaks and acts....Only other travel: riding the rods on freight trains to Duluth and Chicago.

High school art expression limited to posters for Washington High School football games and dances....During summers works with father, now divorced from mother, as gandy dancer on the Masabi Railroad...spends evenings in boxcar camp sketching by light of kerosene lamp the likenesses of section gang workers and the Indian whores who followed the crew.

1942—Drops out of high school to enlist in the army...takes basic training at Camp Callen in San Diego...volunteers for Cook and Bakers' School...learns animal anatomy, chalking and cutting up carcasses of beef, lamb and pig...as army cook prepares meals on the backs of trucks, in field kitchens on the Mojave Desert, on transcontinental troop trains, on the Aquatania troop ship to Europe and through-out England, France and Germany during campaign.

In Europe spends more time painting than ruining GI grub ...paints murals in GI mess halls and swastikas on AA gun barrels in combat zones when enemy planes are shot down.

During Army of Occupation joins Army Special Services as artist doing stage sets and murals for Red Cross Doughnut Dugouts in Germany....Discharged after four years in service—all but one overseas—from Warrington, England, to Pilsen, Czechoslovakia, with five battle stars in ETO,

including the invasion of Normandy, the Ardennes and the Battle of the Bulge, all with the 461st Anti-Aircraft Battalion of the 1st Army.

1946 — Returns to St. Paul, picks up high school credits and studies at the St. Paul Art Center with Clement Haupers, who was a student of André Lhote...studies and paints in the tradition of Cézanne, working mainly with landscape, figure, still life and anatomy....Emphasis on rhythmic composition, scientific color and Cézanne space organization.

In the fall enrolls in the School of the Art Institute of Chicago on the GI Bill....Studies with Boris Anisfeld, a Russian painter who came to the U.S. with the Diaghilev Ballet...introduced to dramatic psychological and emotional color...in school takes keen interest in oriental brushwork....Discovers Dufy and Van Dongen...student work influenced by paintings in large Van Gogh exhibition and exhibition of French tapestries lent to the Art Institute.

First student in fine arts painting program to also study fashion illustration because of his interest in Lautrec, oriental painting and Japanese prints...greatly impressed by Utamaro's grace of line and his album of prints, *The Poem of the Pillow,* and the erotic picture books of the Ukiyo-e artists.

1949 — As third-year student joins faculty to teach figure drawing and fashion illustration...continues to teach for the next 10 years at the Art Institute of Chicago.

Takes academics at University of Chicago, University of Illinois at Navy Pier and DePaul University...exhibits at Minnesota State Fair and South Side Community Art Center in Chicago.

1950—Embarks on multifaceted career of teaching and painting....Illustrates women's high-fashion for Marshall Field and Co., Carson, Pirie, Scott and Co., and Blums-Vogue Stores...thinks of fashion illustration as drawing and watercolor, not merchandising...treats women's millinery like still-life painting with berries, straw, fruit, flowers, ribbon....His elite fashion ads appear in *Vogue, Harper's Bazaar, Glamour, Bride's Magazine.*

Starts sketching Chicago on location: fights at Chicago Stadium; boxers in Johnny Coulon's South Side Gym; horse racing at Arlington, Hawthorne and Sportsman Parks; covers the Cubs, White Sox, Bears and Black Hawks...investigates and sketches Near North Side bars, Rush Street night life, Clark Street strip joints and the luxury yacht basins on the lakefront....His studies of the spectacular Chicago lakefront were to heighten and intensify his color dramatically.

1952—Exhibits for the first time in St. Paul–Minneapolis Twin-City Show at Minneapolis Institute of Arts...wins Chicago Art Directors Award for his high-fashion illustration in ad for Marshall Field and Co.

1953—Paints *Idle Boats,* his first painting using enamel house paints...creates several paintings based on crucifixions, entitled *Homage to Tintoretto* and *Rubens' Crucifixion.* ...Holds first two Chicago area one-man shows....Wins first prize, museum purchase, for *Idle Boats* in Minneapolis Institute of Arts Twin-City Show.

1954—Strong mood of creativity permeates Near North Side of Chicago: action painting, writing and pornography. ...Friend Hugh Hefner launches new magazine called *Playboy* and recruits Neiman to do his first piece for Sep-

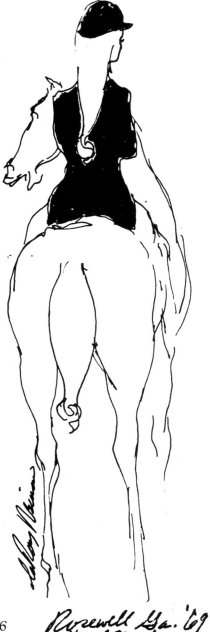

Roswell Ga. '69
Hunt Meet

tember 1954 issue, illustrating a story by Charles Beaumont entitled "Black Country"...this piece wins *Playboy*'s first art prize, awarded by Chicago Art Directors Club Show.

Exhibits in Chicago Artists and Vicinity Show at the Art Institute of Chicago, beginning a run of appearances through 1960.

1955—Teaches painting at Elmwood Park Art League and North Shore Art League (mostly ladies)....Sketches around Chicago's South Side black clubs and jazz joints...for *Chicago Magazine,* sketches Buffalo Bill junket to Cody, Wyoming, with Lucius Beebe...his first *Playboy* cover graces May issue...wins New York Art Directors Show Award for illustration of Beaumont story, "Change of Air," in *Playboy*...show then circulates through Europe....Invited to the Carnegie International Exhibition of oil painting in Pittsburgh—title of painting, *Canyon.*

1956—Very heavy into intellectual art scene in Chicago, participating in panels and seminars, teaching and giving demonstrations...*Pump Room Still Life*, oil painting, is reproduced in September issue of *Town and Country* magazine....Included in "New Talent in America for 1956," published in February 1956 in *Art in America.*

In Chicago's Riverview Amusement Park, became enamored of multicolored merry-go-round, hand-carved by a nineteenth century German wood sculptor...piston motion of horses and rotation of the ride created movement of color that was to make a lasting impression in his work...he painted and drew the gaily colored carrousel again and again during the year.

1957—Teaches landscape painting at School of the Art Institute summer session and painting class at Ox-Bow

Summer School at Saugatuck, Michigan....In June marries Janet Byrne, student at the Art Institute of Chicago....Makes trip for *Playboy* covering great restaurants of San Francisco, Hollywood film-making, gambling in Las Vegas....Exhibits work in Corcoran American Exhibition of oil painting, 25th biannual, Washington, D.C., titled *Chicago Key Club*...represented in 62nd Annual American Exhibition of oil painting, Art Institute of Chicago, with painting titled *Roulette*...painting is reproduced in the *Art Institute Quarterly*....Exhibits *Triptych Carrousel,* oil, in Art Institute Faculty Show....Oil painting, *Pump Room Bar,* wins popular prize in Chicago Artist No-Jury Show, Navy Pier, by vote of 25,000 visitors, and also professional jury award—the Clark Memorial Prize for oil painting...wins same category at Old Orchard Art Festival....Holds one-man show in Chicago and exhibits at Walker Art Center in Minneapolis...appears in half-hour TV special on his work on "Artist's Choice," sponsored by the Art Institute on WTTW.

1958—Illustrates Jack Kerouac's "On the Road" and Budd Schulberg's "A Second Father" for *Playboy*....Spends summer in Los Angeles, San Francisco, Las Vegas....First "Man at His Leisure" feature appears in December issue of *Playboy* on the Pump Room...this feature is to appear regularly for the next 15 years and will take Neiman to the world's most expensive and glamorous social and sporting scenes.

Sketches poets T. S. Eliot and Edith Sitwell in Chicago.... Teaches painting at Ox-Bow Summer School in Saugatuck, Michigan...returns to St. Paul in September to sketch the Flanagan–Aikins fight for St. Paul *Dispatch-Pioneer Press*....Exhibits *Jock,* oil, at ART–USA, Madison Square Garden Show in New York....Wins Hamilton and Graham cash prize at Ball State Teachers College Drawing Show in Muncie, Indiana....Wins Municipal Art Award in Chicago Artists and Vicinity Show with oil painting, *The Bartender*

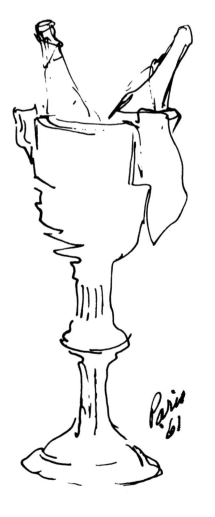

...work is included in USIS Traveling exhibition of 53 Chicago artists to France and Germany...exhibited in Chicago Brotherhood Week Show, also at the Hyde Park Art Center. ...Invited to Society of Contemporary American Art Show at Art Institute of Chicago...also exhibits in Detroit and Philadelphia.

1959—Journeys to Southern Pines, North Carolina, to paint and sketch Moore County Hounds Fox Hunt and Hunter Trials....Queen Elizabeth II admires large charcoal drawing, *Ladies of the Hunt,* while on official visit to Chicago.

Receives purchase prize with oil painting, *Orchestra,* in Mississippi Valley Show at Illinois State Museum, Springfield. ...Exhibits in show, Social Observation and Comment in Art, in Chicago, also in Jazz Exhibition....Shows in the Ringling Museum American Art Exhibition of Oil Painting in Sarasota. ...Holds one-man exhibition of racing scenes at Arlington Park Race Track.

1960—Attends Winter Olympics at Squaw Valley, California, turning on his pens and brushes to the combination of mountain, snow and stretch pants....Takes six-month art trip to Europe for *Playboy,* using as "field studios" such grand hotel suites as Claridge's and the Dorchester in London, Hôtel Georges V in Paris, the Royal Danielli in Venice, the Palace in Madrid, Hôtel de Paris in Monte Carlo, the Carlton in Cannes, Hôtel Negresco in Nice, the Excelsior in Rome....In England, covers Grand National Steeplechase at Aintree; the Cambridge–Oxford Boat Race; Epsom Derby and Ascot Race Meet....In Paris, Maxim's and Tour d'Argent restaurants, Chez Regine, backstage at the Lido and Folies Bergères, polo at Bagatelle, the Steeplechase at Auteuil, racing at Chantilly, the Grand Prix de Paris Horse Race at Longchamp....In southern France—Les Baux restaurant, Saint-Tropez to sketch Bardot, the Cannes Film Festival....On to Fiesta de San

"What's New Pussy cat" '69

Isidro bullfights in Madrid, the Grand Prix in Monaco, and Venice.

Journey also gives first opportunity to see the Goya paintings at the Prado, to travel the Van Gogh and Cézanne landscape country in Arles and Aix-en-Provence, to admire English racing and sporting pictures at the Walker Art Gallery in Liverpool.

Exhibits oil paintings at Des Moines Art Center and the Butler Institute of American Arts at Youngstown, Ohio....Has one-man exhibition of racing paintings at Hialeah Race Course....Invited to Society of Contemporary American Art Exhibition at Art Institute of Chicago.

1961—Takes studio in Paris with Janet, dividing time between Paris and London studio locations....Covers Dublin Horse Show as well as cricket at Lord's in London for sketch feature "The Test," with Alan Ross, in British *Town* magazine....Is interviewed on BBC-TV Monitor comparing the English version of the twist with French counterpart at Chez Regine, which he has been painting.

In France, setting up in the Normandy Hotel at Deauville, sketches the season in full social sway—the casino, polo, racing, boating, golf, tennis, yearling sales, Indian maharajahs, Italian princes, German barons, French counts, English lords, American industrialists, international beauties...motors out from Paris regularly to cover the great restaurants of France with sketchbook...visits and sketches the Champagne country and caves of Reims. ...Returns to Belgium 15 years after the Battle of the Bulge and sketches action at casino in Knokke...in cathedral at Antwerp sees the *Erection of the Cross* by Rubens, which he had copied from a small reproduction eight years before in Chicago....Spends much time at La Galerie des Batailles (Hall of Battles) at Versailles.

COLONY SPORTING CLUB

CASINO

and

RESTAURANT

BERKELEY SQUARE, LONDON, W.1
Telephone: MAYfair 657/8/9

2 July, 1966

...Studies paintings and drawings of Napoleon around Paris, *The Lady with the Unicorn* tapestries at the Musée de Cluny in Paris and Fragonard's wash drawings at the Petit Palais in Paris....Has one-man show in Chicago and wins gold medal for oil painting at the Salon d'Art Moderne in Paris.

1962—Sketches through the Bordeaux wine country vineyards and châteaux. Sketches the Giraglia Yacht Race sailing from San Remo to Toulon, also the Regatta of the Gondoliers in Venice. Moves on to Florence and Rome, joining Fellini on the set of *8½*. Sketches Gina Lollobrigida on the movie sets at Cine Citta in Rome. Flies back to the States to cover Indianapolis 500 on commission to execute twelve paintings of the auto race.

Sketches at Dior and St. Laurent openings in Paris. Covers Carryback, America's entry in the Grand Prix de Paris, including training at Chantilly. Collaborates with Art Buchwald on *Paris-Match* feature "Y a-t-il des Playboys?" May 1962. Does special feature of paintings for "Turn of the Twist," article in *About Town* magazine, London, March 1962.

In course of travels admire's Hogarth's works, including *Rake's Progress* and *Harlot's Delight* in London, and in Venice, at Scoula Grande de San Rocco, Tintoretto's *Crucifixion,* which he had interpreted in 1953 in Chicago, and at Palazzo Labia Tiepolo's allegorical fresco *I Banchetto de Antonia e Cleopatra.* Has one-man shows in London and Paris.

On January 1, 1963, returns from Paris to establish studio in New York. Takes trip to Mexico with Shel Silverstein; they sketch Mexico City bull ring, Acapulco resort scene. Returns to Indianapolis for 500. In the course of this first year in New York goes on junket with Jerry Lewis to Canada; teaches

Prince Philip
Windsor '64

LeRoy Neiman

painting at Ox-Bow Summer School at Saugatuck; conducts painting classes at Arts and Crafts, Winston-Salem, North Carolina; sketches at Yankee Stadium and Monmouth Park and Atlantic City racetracks; covers the Fire Island scene and New York belly dancers. Also sketches Hugh Hefner's obscenity trial in Chicago. Paints mural *Homage to Lautrec* and supervises installation in the Continental Hotel in Chicago. Has one-man show at Hammer Gallery in New York, exhibits at Galerie 18, Paris.

Spends February 1964 in Miami Beach covering training and pre-fight drama of Cassius Clay–Sonny Liston fight. Liston verbally throws him out of training area because Neiman refuses to discard unlit cigar. Sketches ringside at fight. During Miami stay, Hialeah racetrack provides special private, flower-covered studio at the track.

Meets Linda Moreno, who is to be his studio assistant for next 10 years, at Sir John's Cuban Club. Sketches New York Yankees at spring training in Fort Lauderdale. In New York, sketches rehearsals for musical *Golden Boy* and does portrait of Sammy Davis, Jr. as Golden Boy used for souvenir program cover. Does drawings for *Harper's* magazine article "Cassius Clay and Malcolm X," by George Plimpton, June 1964.

Journeys to Stockholm for Eddie Machen–Floyd Patterson fight....In London looks in on and sketches Crockford's, the Colony and River Club casinos, polo at Windsor with Prince Philip, fights at Wembley Stadium and Café Royal. ...Flies to Paris to cover the Tour de France bike race. ...Covers the America Cup yacht race at Newport, Rhode Island, sketching America's entry, *Constellation,* crews and spectator fleet....Buys a point of heavyweight Oscar Bonavena....Sketches at Santa Anita race course in Los Angeles....Exhibits oil painting at New York World's Fair,

*Jockey in the Colors of Guy de Rothschild....*Shows paintings at Galleria Fiorentina d'Arte, Florence, Italy.

1965—Executes twelve 8' x 4' paintings for Playboy Resort Hotel in Jamaica on theme of dance variations....Neiman does hundreds of paintings for 18 Playboy clubs that open between 1960-1970....Has one-man show of paintings on a French theme at the French Center, Astor Tower Gallery in Chicago....John Carr hosts educational TV special based on Neiman's work in second solo show at Hammer Gallery, New York....Covers the Clay–Liston fight at Lewiston, Maine, and does second sketchbook on Ali fights....Life-size painting, 8' x 6', of Sugar Ray Robinson, shown at Madison Square Garden on night of Sugar's "Farewell to Boxing," stolen and never recovered....Attends Meadow Brook Christmas Hunt on December 24 to do special painting commission....Charcoal drawing, *Pissotière,* published in *Paris Review...*Fascinated with Marianne Moore's Napoleonic tri-corner chapeau, Neiman does series of drawings of the poetess.

1966—Paints 8' x 56' mural, *Afternoon on the Indiana Dunes,* and supervises installation in the Mercantile National Bank in Hammond, Indiana....Attends Kentucky Derby and paints Graustark, Derby Dan Farm's injured favorite....Paints basketball player Cazzie Russell on commission for 12-year-old fan in Michigan.

Stays three months in London executing all paintings for the London Playboy Club....Sketches portraits of personalities around London—Kenneth Tynan, Bader Mulla, David Frost, Clement Freud, Sir Ralph Richardson, Woody Allen, Douglas Fairbanks, Robert Morley, Prince Merid Beyene of Ethiopia, Ursula Andress, the Beatles and "Birds of London" series....Sketches at Murray's Cabaret, Dolly's Disco, Newmarket and Soho spots, Wimbledon and "Trooping of the Colors."...Does collage for film *Casino Royale,* also painting that is subsequently stolen from theater on the night of movie's New York premiere.

Returns to States in midsummer to sketch and paint California surfing from San Diego, San Ofre to Malibu....Sketches the disco sounds at Ondine, Le Club and Cheetah in New York....Paints Cassius Clay for cover of *Ring* magazine—a sentimental gesture because *Ring* has been boxing Bible of childhood.

In New York studies Unicorn tapestries at the Cloisters and the great tapestries at the Metropolitan Museum....Completes special sketches for TV coverage of National Horse Show....Swedish Lloyd Company commissions him to paint 4' x 24' mural, *Ascot,* for S.S. *Patricia.*

1967—Sketches Leonard Bernstein at rehearsal in Philharmonic Hall, also the Millrose Games track meet at Madison Square Garden....Paints polo at Oak Brook, Illinois. ...Collaborates with Muhammad Ali on prediction painting for Zora Folley fight, after morning run with Ali around reservoir in Central Park....Does TV credit sketches for Ali-Folley fight, also TV sketches for Griffith-Benvenuti fight coverage....September *Esquire* magazine publishes article on Muhammad Ali, drawings done for and with LeRoy Neiman.

Spends six weeks with Frank Sinatra at the Fontainebleau in Miami on the *Tony Rome* set, also on New York set of *The Detective....*Completes series of humorous watercolors of Mark Twain surfing for a TV script based on Twain's surfing essays....Sketches Suzanne Farrell of New York City ballet during rehearsal of *Don Quixote.*

Spends three days in the Ford pits at LeMans 24-hour endurance auto race in France....Revisits Rome for a look at its night life....Paints Piazza del Populo and then the Via

Veneto from roof of the Hotel Flora. Holds exhibition in Florence and returns once again to Venice. Drives to Yugoslavia and lives as nudist to cover the nudist colony scene from the Istrian peninsula along the Dalmation Islands to Dubrovnik and Sveti Stefan. Sketches the bullfights at Plaza Monumental in Barcelona on way to Pamplona to cover the Fiesta de San Fermin. Tops off the Pamplona stay by actually running with the bulls.

Goes to Bridgeport, Connecticut, with New York Jets for Jet Huddle TV show. Travels with the Jets entire football season

Painting Playboy Playmate Ellen Michaels in Neiman's New York studio 1974

and sits on the bench as "artist-in-residence." Does quick portrait of Hank Aaron on pregame TV show at Shea Stadium with Don Criqui. Does poster for the Daytona 500.

Visits the Cowboy Museum in Oklahoma City and receives an award from the Oklahoma City Art Directors Club. Goes to New Haven to catch the "tail-gating" scene at Yale Bowl during Yale–Harvard football game. Has two one-man shows in New York. Paints mural, *Hunt of the Unicorn,* and supervises installation in Playboy Resort Hotel at Lake Geneva, Wisconsin. Rounds out year by sketching New Year's Eve at El Morocco in New York.

Early in 1968 flies to Montreal to sketch Bobby Hull for March *Time* magazine cover and does twenty-five comprehensive-from-life sketches for painting.

Flies off on painting trip to Russia. En route sketches at Royal Golf Club in Brussels....Sketches the Bolshoi Opera and Ballet, also Russian synagogue during Passover season. ...Takes in the youth scene in Moscow, sketching at Youth Cafés....Honored at Peace Society meeting and sits on dais with Aram Khachaturian and other Russian art luminaries. ...Draws backstage at the Kirov Ballet in Leningrad. ...After Russian trip gets caught up in ballet and sketches Rudolf Nureyev at Lincoln Center.

Drawings of Benvenuti–Griffith fight appear as black-and-white spread in the Italian magazine *Boxe-Ring*....Does stint sketching strippers at Minsky's in Mineola, L.I., and in Manhattan, including special series on Candy Barr at the Gayety Theater.

Starts teaching art class for Atlanta Youth Council in Atlanta poverty program, commuting monthly to Georgia. ...Makes series of drawings of soccer great, Pelé, in Atlanta and again at Yankee Stadium.

Does pen-and-ink of Bobby Kennedy for *Harper's* magazine article, "Travels with Bobby Kennedy," by David Halberstam. ...Shocked by assassination of RFK, he is moved to do special etching from drawings done from life....Etching is printed in limited edition in Switzerland in 1971.

Visits Whitney estate, Greentree, to sketch court tennis. ...As artist-in-residence, gets involved in Jetmania as team pursues football championship....Has special showing of Jet drawings and paintings done for Jet Huddle TV Show at Hammer Gallery.

Does ink drawing of Chicago's Mayor Richard Daley for article "Jowl to Jowl" by Studs Terkle for *Law and Disorder,* special documentary magazine published on the circumstances and incidents of the 1968 Democratic Presidential Convention in Chicago.

Does special ink drawings for *Harper's* magazine article "In the Faraway Country of Montgomery, Alabama," by Almena Lomax.

1969 — In January sketches from the bench at Orange Bowl as New York Jets win the Super Bowl....Draws Edward Villella as Harlequin in *Harlequinade* at New York City Ballet several times during season.

In Atlanta, sketches Martin Luther King, Sr., in office of Ebenezer Church; Mayor Ivan Allen and Governor Lester Maddox in their offices; also Julian Bond and pitcher Juan Marichal, who model for poverty program painting classes. ...Covers Hunt and Steeplechase Meet at Rosewell, Georgia. ...Paints Robert Shaw conducting the Atlanta Symphony, and sketches Senator Ted Kennedy for the LeRoy Neiman's

"Atlantans" feature in *Atlanta* magazine....Does film credit art for *Pussycat, Pussycat, I Love You.* Does art for *Oh! Calcutta,* musical in New York City, also poster for *Whores, Wars and Tin Pan Alley,* Kurt Weill inspiration.

Painting of Abraham Lincoln, commissioned by Lincoln scholar and historian Ralph Newman, is reproduced on the cover of the Chicago *Tribune* Sunday magazine....Also pen drawings of Greek shipping czars Onassis, Niarchos and Pappas for the *Wall Street Journal....*Creates sports mural for Iron Horse Restaurant in Madison Square Garden depicting New York teams in action....Exhibits at National Portrait Gallery, Washington, D.C., in *Time* magazine cover show.

Takes off for Morocco trip via Lisbon....Sketches and paints through Casablanca, Rabat, Agadir, Tangiers—including belly dancers of Katoubia Palace...even camel races.

Collaborates with Dave Anderson on book *Countdown to Super Bowl,* featuring sketches and cover painting....Appears as regular on Jet Huddle TV show and Namath TV show, starting another season as the Jets' artist-in-residence. ...Attends Jets game with Larry Merchant, writing story on assignment for *Jock* magazine entitled, "Oh, How LeRoy Suffers for His Art."...Merchant discovers Shea Stadium Neiman cheering section: when the Jets are behind, fans yell, "Put LeRoy in!"

Sketches James Brown at the Apollo....Exhibits at Minnesota Museum of Art in St. Paul (first time in hometown in 15 years).

1970—Starts off with special commission for the Fifth Dimension singing group, large painting and sketches used for album cover....Also sketches Sly and the Family Stone at Madison Square Garden....Does poster and charcoal portrait of Brendan Behan, work used in Broadway production of *Borstal Boy,* Tony Award winner as year's best dramatic play.

Visits the New York Stock Exchange to do several on-the-spot drawings and watercolors of the action on the floor. ...Flies to Dublin for exhibition of drawings at Abbey Theater....Sketches the horse races during Curragh Meet, also Dublin dog tracks and Phoenix Park races....Flies to Montreal to attend and sketch the Can-Am auto race....Commissioned to paint portrait of Pancho Gonzales that is presented to the tennis hero as "Grandfather of the Year." ...Sketches at cockfight training camp in hills of Jamaica.

Joins Hugh Hefner on Big Black Bunny Jet for trip to Europe and Africa...in course of trip visits London, Marbella, Bengazi, Khartoum, Nairobi, Kenya (on safari), Rome, Venice, Munich, Paris, Rabat and cruises Greek Islands.

Back in New York, sketches Pirates-Mets baseball game in afternoon, Giants-Bears football game in evening...also documents the World Series in sketches for baseball commissioner's office....For book, *This Great Game,* paints dozen of baseball's $100,000 players....Creates poster for Ali-Quarry fight in Atlanta....Captures in drawings the mind-blowing pre-fight scene at the Regency Hotel...after fight, appears on ABC's "Wide World of Sports" with Ali and Howard Cosell....National Football League magazine, *Pro,* features "Neiman on Namath" sketches.

Has one-man show in New York at Hammer Gallery....Felicie Schumsky visits studio for first time to discuss printmaking.

1971—Involvement deepens with the heralded Ali-Frazier fight...does official fight program, widely distributed fight poster and special paintings for press kit, including rendition of the championship belt....Drawing of Ali adorns cover of

Bar
Grand Hotel
Stockholm
'64

New York Times Sunday magazine....Sketches Joe Frazier at the Concord and runs with him in 11-below weather. ...Sketches Ali in training in Miami....After fight, *Twen*, a German magazine, uses drawings for their fight coverage. ...Produces portfolio of 15 etchings of the fight....Returns as guest artist on "Wide World of Sports," featuring fight postmortem with Ali.

Flies with the New York Yankees from Miami to Caracas for exhibition games....Journeys to London and sketches Sotheby's auction rooms for *Playboy* feature....Covers the race meets at Longchamp.

Develops interest in printmaking and creates first series of lithographs at Matthieu in Dielsdorf, Switzerland....Does etchings at Atelier Weber in Zurich for Orangerie Verlag, Cologne, using suite at the Grand Dolder Hotel to work on copper plates during summer residence....In Monte Carlo displays pre-fight sketches of Benvenuti and Monzon on ABC's "Wide World of Sports."

Sketches Canonero II, Venezuelan thoroughbred, at Belmont Park, and appears on CBS pre-race telecast for Belmont Stakes....Does two-part TV program on the art of lithography....Starts series of silk screens for Jack Solomon. ...Returns to London to sketch Ascot race meet....In Paris, with Felicie, sketches French jockey Yves St. Martin at his home in Lamorlaye and while riding at Longchamp....Illustrates José Torres' book, *Sting Like a Bee*....Sketches the Ali–Jimmy Ellis fight in Houston for the *National Observer*. ...Spends month on location painting mural for the Playboy Resort Hotel at Great Gorge, New Jersey, *Harlequin's Entrance into Venice*, 4' x 103'....Several paintings are included in *Playboy* traveling exhibition to Europe and the Orient.

1972—Creates Super Bowl cover for *Time* magazine. ...Sketches Super Bowl action from the bench in New

At the Royal Ascot, 1971

*With Jack Nicklaus, Doral
Country Club, Florida, 1973*

*With Reggie Jackson,
World Series, 1972*

Orleans....Joins Bob Considine in radio show at Patterson-Bonavena fight....Sketches pro basketball championship game between Knicks and Lakers in Los Angeles Forum for silk-screen print and etching....Shows hockey sketches on NBC-TV coverage of Rangers–Canadiens at Madison Square Garden....Sketches Yogi Berra on camera in Mets' dugout for CBS-TV news....Starts series of studies of the massage parlors and prostitute scene on 42nd Street.

Spends a month on Long Island looking over the Hamptons summer scene for *Playboy*....In Atlanta, sketches the All-Star baseball game....Covers the Fischer–Spassky world championship chess match in Reykjavik, Iceland, as sole visual reporter for ABC's "Wide World of Sports" when no cameras are allowed....Draws Jack Nicklaus at Westchester Classic golf tournament for serigraph and *Golf Digest* cover.

Flies to Munich to cover all aspects of the 1972 Olympics for ABC, his work seen by 80 million viewers....Sketches World Series for NBC, appearing on Joe Garagiola pregame show....Has special charity showing of Olympic drawings at "21" Club in New York, where two drawings are stolen and never recovered....Goes to Ottawa for appearance in film, *Wrestling Queen,* and gets tossed on elbow by 315-pound wrestler, Mad Dog Vachon, while scuffling over sketchbook in rigged, but unrehearsed, skit...develops tennis elbow as injury lingers.

On commission, sketches prize show horse, Hot Fudge, at National Horse Show for later development into painting. ...Appears in TV coverage of the International Horse Race at Laurel, Maryland, for independent producer Tommy Roberts....Opens exhibition of Olympic sketches and paintings at the Indianapolis Museum of Art....Creates football cover and feature paintings for *Newsweek* for running backs article by Pete Axthelm....Has one-man exhibition of drawings at Museo de Bellas Artes, Caracas, with enthusiastic

Ethel Kennedy, Far Gallery, New York, 1971

student response, and one-man show of paintings at Hammer Gallery in New York.

1973—Attends Super Bowl and joins Joe Namath and Curt Gowdy in pregame telecast on NBC from Newport Beach, California....Sketches the George Foreman–Joe Frazier fight in Jamaica, also the illegal gambling games in Kingston.... In Detroit, does NBC guest shot with Tim Ryan on Stanley Cup hockey coverage....Makes personal-appearance tour with traveling show of Olympic prints from California to Washington, D.C....At the Masters golf tourney in Augusta, sketches Arnold Palmer in the rain for *Golf Digest*....Paints Babe Ruth memorial painting for baseball commissioner Bowie Kuhn....Sketches thoroughbred, Secretariat, at Belmont workouts and develops paintings later, then publishes special serigraph.

Sketches oldsters in old people's homes for *National Lampoon* parody on himself....Paints homage to Frederic Remington, and also creates serigraph of same subject....Does pen, ink and wash study of Dizzy Gillespie and Charlie Parker for Museum of Jazz poster, and another of Benny Goodman.

Curator of prints of Hermitage Museum, Leningrad, selects 19 silk-screens for the permanent collection and exhibition, for which Neiman does special poster....Paints life-size Ali figure on wall of gym at Muhammad Ali training camp in Deer Lake, Pennsylvania....Does football pen-and-ink drawings for the *New York Times'* pregame report on Jets vs. Giants....Covers "California on Wheels" scene from Berkeley to Los Angeles, looking in on the Hell's Angels and other wheel cultures.

Acts as artist-at-large for ABC coverage of Bobby Riggs–Billie Jean King tennis match at the Houston Astrodome ...sketches also appear in the *New York Times*....Finishes film short about his mural, *Harlequin's Entrance into Venice*.

With Johnny Bench,
Cincinnati, 1971

With Joe Namath, Shea
Stadium, 1969

Painting mural of Muhammad Ali at Ali's camp in Deer Lake, Pennsylvania. '73

LeRoy Neiman 1974 art calendar is designed and distributed. ...Has one-man shows of prints and drawings from coast to coast: Circle Galleries in New York, Dallas, Chicago, Los Angeles, San Francisco; Brentano's in Boston, Beverly Hills, New York; Palm Beach Gallery in Palm Beach, Florida; Saratoga Gallery in Saratoga, New York; University of Illinois, Urbana; and University of Texas, Austin; also Cadaques Gallery in Cadaques, Spain....Graphic work is represented by some 500 galleries in the United States as well as Sweden, Canada, Japan, England and France.

Serves as NBC's guest artist for Dallas–Oakland Thanksgiving Day game, and for Dallas–Miami pro football playoff on New Year's Eve, with Curt Gowdy.

1974—Flies to London to sketch the Whatton Fox Hunt near Tring for a commission of 15 oil paintings....Does pen-and-ink sketches preceding the Ali–Frazier Super Fight II of January 28, 1974, which appear in Sunday *New York Times*...also does pre-fight sketches analyzing fighters for Howard Cosell show with George Foreman.

Exhibition of prints, drawings and paintings held at the Springfield Museum in Springfield, Massachusetts, through month of February....Covers Stanley Cup playoffs with sketches for NBC....Starts Boxing Sketchbook, featuring 12 fights in 10 years, to be published by Felicie, Inc., and printed at Draeger Frères, Paris....Does 12 paintings for deluxe book of Melville's *Moby Dick,* with foreword by Jacques Cousteau, to be published by The Artist's Limited Edition, and printed at the press of A. Colish, Inc....Atlanta Film Festival, in September, is commemorated by Neiman poster....Accepts commission to do painting for the Newport Jazz Festival poster.

Has one man show in Tokyo sponsored by Sony. In Zaïre acts as official artist for Ali-Foreman fight promotion with solo exhibition in Kinshasa.

SKETCHBOOK ... *with artist's notes*

The English possess an historical fondness for appearing taller than they are (when they need to feel formidable)...as witness the elevated headpieces of the English Bobby, the Palace Guard and the proper gentleman on formal social patrol...in costumes largely unchanged for generations...theirs is a vertical society...even the buses are taller...no other culture has this particular vanity, with the possible exception of certain African tribes I have sketched on sa-

There is a strength that attaches to great English architecture which endures and survives that of other cultures it has influenced ...many 19th century buildings in the American east, inspired by British design, have long since yielded to the bulldozer...but in London the stately British structures still stand, undisturbed by war or time.

view from
45 PARK LANE
Hyde Park corner
6-7-66
LeRoy Neiman

fari...the average London bloke takes up more space than necessary...wearing the maximum amount of haberdash, at all seasons, in all weather...plus skillful urban use of the ever-required umbrella...subjects of the crown refuse to be embarrassed by rain ...and are encouraged by the example of the Queen, who manages her own umbrella.

The true test of traditional British reserve is traditional British traffic...from the sleekly silent Rolls-

105

PERMANENT BUILDING SOCIETY

BARCLAY'S BANK LIMITED

LeRoy Neiman
Dorchester Hotel London 6?

PARK LANE

Park Lane
from The Dorchester
March 1960

Royce to the sturdy London taxi ...on foot, each morning, the British professional class strolls across London Bridge on its way to work...all in bowlers...carrying umbrellas and attaché cases... their uniform progress distracted only by an occasional glimpse of a leggy British bird....In 1966, for the opening of the London Playboy Club, I did a series of inspired sketches of English dollies in their world-sweeping, mind-blowing fashion discovery, the miniskirt... the advent of the mini and its later refinement, the micro—fashion's version of the atom and H-bombs— represented a breakthrough...today's English women are the most exciting in the world, proof of which is the fact that their government scandals are always so much more interesting than ours.

'66

London Leroy Neiman

Westminster
Abbey

4 June '66

LeRoy Neiman

BUNKER
Control Center
Churchill's Hide

Trooping of
the Colours
6-66

Ascot

In the costume of high occasion, the British peerage and aristocratic rich move toward waiting limousines for the drive—a pilgrimage, really—18 miles west of London...their ladies are a bouquet of colors in satin and ceremonial brocades...and brandish oversized chapeaux created for the occasion...a crown tradition since 1711, celebrated in the lyrics of *My Fair Lady*, The Royal Ascot is a legacy of elegance past ...the social and sporting highlight of British turfdom...to emphasize the special aura of the four-day meet, the Queen departs Windsor Castle by carriage to open each day's program...when the Queen arrives the gents instantly become shorter...they remove their toppers. To the proud jockey posturing in the paddock, his conformation is as important

Ascot

PIGGOTT

artist proof   LeRoy Neiman

On June 14, 1972, Lester Piggott rode at Brighton in the afternoon, at Leicester in the evening and was in the irons for the first race at Ascot on June 15.

as that of the horse...his attitude suggests a tolerance of the aristocratic idleness around him...the jockeys are like tulips on horseback...and appear inordinately in love with their role...artists have long been fascinated with the horse and the way of life it has come to represent...ironically, Géricault died in a spill at age 33 ...his contemporary Decamps died the same way...and Lautrec was crippled in yet another equestrian fall.

The Englishman upper class born at the top keen socially fit

Leaving the Dorchester for the Royal Ascot Second day 1966 LeRoy Neiman

The flow of the swells from the royal enclosure to the paddock and back reflects the social ladder on parade...earls, dukes, M.P.'s, dilettantes and their wives—or surrogate wives—all making the timeless foot march to perform their visual research for the next race...the procession assumes the air of a combination Victorian lawn party and period fashion showing...the class structure, established centuries ago, is much in evidence ...top hats are de rigueur in the royal enclosure and admission is by invitation only... it is a montage of finery and form ...film celebrities and Mayfair models...merchants attired by Moss Brothers...titled elite and young rakes...with the security of manner and speech and dress assured by position and bloodline ...the Royal Box is surrounded by courtiers...generating an endless exchange of pleasantries and bows, while loyal and admiring subjects look on...the first four rows of the paddock are dominated by ladies, the dowagers and the ambitious...a veritable hen party of the rightly born...a piece of the tapestry of Ascot, a bit threadbare but still colorful.

Winners enclosure

ROYAL ASCOT
1960

Second Day

10,000
champagne
rks popped
in 4-day meet

1971
British democracy—
on His Form—
3 English—
owned horses—
are named:
Ballet Banaein
Waterloo
Phillip of Spain

LeRoy Neiman
63

the Royal Procession
June 16 '71
the Queen and Prince Phillip
Princess Ann

Gold Cup Day '71

In those fine, preening moments in the walking ring, before and between races, horse, jockey and throng become one, a kind of theater in the oval...the rustle of foliage, the soft footsteps of horses being led, are the only sounds that escape...the only discordant sartorial note is the less splendid, but serviceable garb of the lads leading the steeds..."I sty in rycing," a cockney hot walker told me, "because you get next to the rich. If you rub shoulders with the rich, some of it 'as to rub off"...at Ascot, little suggests that it does....When the usual race-day rain falls gently, one lady fair observes, "We've seen horses, now let's get into the dry" ...after the rain the washed grass is greener...the emotions of the race-goers rise in proportion to how many pounds have been wagered...the lathered horses, with flared and bleeding nostrils, follow the white rail to the finish ...then the vast assemblage tenders an ovation of polite applause to the winner.

Horseracing

For me in a changing world there are three reliables: the Catholic church, any graphics workshop and the racetrack...the service and language are the same whatever the country...no problem with currency, either...horse racing is truly the sport of kings— and rogues...every track is laid out to lure the flock...you feel very welcome....Whether sketching the Grand National at Aintree or the run for the roses at Churchill Downs, the color, beauty, movement and pageantry, the imperial quality of it, are the same...here man and beast are partners...a small, wiry, harlequin figure, the jockey is required to control a quarter ton of high-strung horseflesh...in a demanding trade, they are tough and vain...women jockeys have no more vanity than the male...he is the peacock of the paddock, primping and combing in the tack room between races. The colors of the silks are crucial to the progress of the race... numbers are no longer visible when the horses are bunched, but

LeRoy Neiman '72

Belmont Park N.Y.
May 29 71
Stable Area
Barn 7A
Stall 14

Canonero II
Juan Quintero
groom

Frank Starnes
Blacksmith

French
Jock
Longchamp

the sophisticated, field-glassed observer will isolate the color of his choice as the field flashes along ...this celebration of colors is in contrast to the quiet, early morning hues of Newmarket, where the English train their thoroughbreds on the misty heath...for centuries a favorite scene in British sporting prints...those who run do so before breakfast...and the artist must rise early to observe a Secretariat or a Joe Frazier or a Frank Shorter...at gallop.

Nal Turcotte
Canada
Braulio Baeza
Panama
Buster Parnell
Ireland
Willie Shoemaker
USA
Lester Piggott
England
Yuji Nohira
Japan
Jean Cruguet
France

Jockey Room
Laurel Race Course
Washington D.C. International 10-11-72

Urinals in jockey room
are lower

Colors of
A Aga Khan

Baron Guy
de Rothschild

Laurel Race Course
Maryland 1973

Maisons - Laffitte

Jockey Room
Built 1886
HUNTING LODGE

17 June '64 Newmarket Heath LeRoy Neiman

Koog and Yogi, Shea Stadium '66

LeRoy Neiman

Manteaux

There is a nakedness about the preliminary fighter, the shopworn veteran, who enters the ring wearing a faded, frayed robe...he is visibly self-conscious...unlike the life-class model who mounts the platform with a certain pride and slips out of her robe...the status of the fighter is often measured by the length of his robe, which, once shed, signals he is ready for work ...civilized people spend a monotonous part of life getting into and out of topcoats, coats, jackets, capes...the family of robes.

*Man getting into coat
Paris Opera*

LeRoy Neiman '59

Emile Griffith LeRoy Neuman
Madison Sq Garden
N.Y.

LeRoy Neuman
'73

Wheels

The notebooks of da Vinci reveal a fascination with the wheels of the chariot...today all the world turns on wheels...the pedestrian kibitzer, who gets a natural high peering into the limousine, ignores the chauffeur to investigate who is in back...there the VIP relaxes, the wheel of the cassette spinning in his tape deck...the luxury limo is the rich man's camper...the interior contains everything essential to his world...stereo, TV, bar, telephone, chick...and is never subjected to the family car pile-in.

Indy '61

LeRoy Neiman Gasoline Alley

7 A.M.

CHAIKA
(sea gull) ..... Moscow

*Oriental Rug
Curtained Windows*

LeRoy Neiman
3-7a-68

Hef's new limo
Feb. '67
LeRoy Neiman   CHICAGO

LeRoy Neiman
'73 Regency Hotel, N.Y.

130

LeRoy Neiman Monte Carlo '71

New York cabbies use the interior of their cabs for self-expression and advertising — a Times Square influence.

CHEER UP thing could be worse you could have my job!

UNITED TAXI OWNERS GUILD

DRIVER SENSITIVE TO SMOKE PLEASE CO-OPERATE

KLEENEX

THIS CAB OPERATES OUT OF CITY LIMITS ASK DRIVER FOR SPECIAL RATES

USE ASHTRAYS OR DON'T SMOKE DON'T THROW LITTER ON FLOOR

PLEASE KEEP NEW YORK CLEAN USE ASHTRAYS TREAT MY TAXI AS YOUR OWN

PLEASE DO NOT SLAM DOOR

POLICE CALL M 0 289

NOV. PAGE 1 2 3 4 5 6 7 8 9 10 11 12 13

PLEASE USE ASHTRAYS

FARE

TAXI CAB

NO U TURN PERMITTED

CAB N°5 EXPIRES MAY 31 16

YOU ARE RESPONSIBLE FOR THE SAFE OPERATION OF THIS VEHICLE

NOTICE TO PASSENGERS YOUR DRIVER

REMINDER — TAKE YOUR PROPERTY

COUGHING AND SNEEZING ARE CONTAGIOUS AND INJUROUS. KINDLY COVER THEM. IT IS ALSO RIGHT AND PROPER

PLEASE KEEP YOUR FEET ON THE FLOOR

THE LAW DON'T SLAM DOOR

CAUTION KINDLY WATCH YOUR HANDS WHEN CLOSING DOOR. this cab accepts out of town t

Scull's Angels Two W57 Radio

PLEASE SIT BACK IN CASE OF SHORT STOP FOR YOUR OWN SAFETY

PLEASE CO-OPERATE WITH THIS DRIVER TO AVOID BOTTLENECKS. HAVE YOUR FARE READY BEFORE REACHING YOUR DESTINATION

THE LAW PASSENGERS MUST USE CURB SIDE DOORS ONLY

DOOR HAN

PASSENGERS MUST PAY ALL TOLLS BRIDGES AND TUNNELS

NO SPITTING ON FLOOR

LeRoy Neiman New York 66-72

88

GOODYEAR

Gulf

Dan Gurney

6-27 '70 Linda powders her nose

Mont Tremblant Canada

Can-Am Race June 27 '70

LeRoy Neiman

out Mont Tremblant Canada

131

France '67

Start at Indy '62

Can-Am Pits '70
mont Tremblant
Canada

Not only great artists and international playboys die in car crashes —so do auto racers....The public delights in reading about or, better yet, witnessing a sensational gangland slaying....A restaurant can gain popularity because it was host to a mobster being gunned down while dining.

These demonstrations of mob warfare are not the only romantic, spectacular spectator deaths that hold the fancy of the public... sports also contribute with auto racing, as well as sky diving or bull fighting.

Auto racing is indeed romantic and exotic. Today's drivers are athletes as well as daredevils....The pits are made elegant by the international flavor of many languages —Swedish, Portuguese, French, Italian, Spanish and English.

Ernie's
San Francisco
LeRoy Neiman
Dec 12, '65

Haute Cuisine

I feel a debt to the artist who drew the face on the barroom floor... and to the impoverished bohemian artist who sketched on the table-cloth to pay for the price of a meal ...they made it acceptable for me to carry my implements into bars and restaurants without offending form or tradition...I favor the haute cuisine establishments, where the maître d' is even more snobbish than the well-heeled guests he serves...and the appearance of the chef from the galley generates the same excitement as a movie star entering the foyer ...the literature of the menu features print so fine that it seems another attempt by management to intimidate the diner and make him put on his glasses.

le Carlton RESTAURANT

boulevard de Waterloo, Bruxelles 1
Tél.: 12.30.40 (5 lignes)
PARKING ASSURE
SALONS PRIVES
JARDIN D'ETE
SERVICE TRAITEUR

Coupant le Jambon d'Ardenne

LeRoy Neiman 3-23-'68

"21" 2-18-'70
Aristotle Onassis

2 wine stewards
2 waiters

Waiting for Ari
The Big Trip   2:50 P.M.

Top celebs are seen and photographed so often at restaurants, bars and resorts, an image builds, that this is all they do. We are startled to find them anywhere else.

THE STAGS HEAD
The Stags Head
Dame Court Dublin
LeRoy Neiman   Aug 10, 1961

Louis Prosser

SBM MONTE CARLO
CARTE DES VINS

SBM MONTE CARLO

HOTEL DE PARIS

Black Turtle and Wet look vinyl

Monte Carlo
Empire Room
Hotel De Paris
LeRoy Neiman

Monzon at Dinner

Thurs May 6,'71
Middleweight Champion Carlos
Monzon's training table.
His wine is Portuguese

Toots Shor
Monday nite
Sept 29'69

LeRoy Neiman

Dick Andrew   Considine   Breslin   Jack Price

The beer drinker

138

Mother and Son lunching at the Beach Club Southhampton '71

gran
Café de Paris
Tangier

La Coupole
102 Blvd Montparnasse
Paris
Paris
'65
LeRoy Neiman

L'Escale
ST. TROPEZ

LeRoy Neiman Rome

WORKING
PRESS

WORLD'S HEAVYWEIGHT CHAMPIONSHIP FIGHT
LISTON vs. CLAY
MIAMI BEACH CONVENTION HALL
TUE., FEB. 25, 1964, 8:45 P. M.
NEIMAN
Play Boy
THIS IS YOUR ADMISSION TICKET
Non-Transferable

ENTER PRESS
N° 171   GATE No. 2
— ONLY —
(Southeast Side of Convention Hall)
W D 19

Big Fights

Hot blood turns cold when first blood is drawn...one corner man always used a red towel so his fighter couldn't see his own blood ...didn't want to discourage the lad...a blood sport, a once Catholic-dominated sport...once fighters genuflected, now they try to psych each other out with baleful stares ...when a Catholic fought a Jewish kid it was the New Testament versus the Old...today it is the black against the Hispanic...they share the same sociological predicament...the display of public emotion at the end of a fight— embracing after they have bloodied each other—reflects this ethnic awareness...at that moment a feeling close to love passes between them.

Roadwork
Feb 2 '71
around lake
3 miles

Joe
Frazier

Ken Norton

11° below

Temperature 11°

Depart 5:25   return 6:05
Concord Hotel   A.M.   A.M.   below
                                 zero

Clay's training Quarters 5th St. Gym
Wed. Feb. 5, 64   Miami Beach   LeRoy Neiman

There is a moment in every career when the hot young fighter is beautiful...and he knows it at instructions before the fight in the center of the ring...every hair slicked in place...his body shines as his handler kneads the shoulders ...he nods at his friends in the crowd...the glamour of the moment charges all...if he could quit at that point he would be handsome the rest of his life...but there is about him a fragile quality... vulnerable...it is magnified, that look, when he loses...six fights too many will make a difference... unless he is an Ali, he's six fights away from making that turn, becoming marked....When Ali, as Cassius Clay, faced Sonny Liston, he physically overshadowed him and added inches to his height by bouncing on his toes in the corner before the bell...but the crowd, still awed by Liston's jailbird legend, didn't notice.

At big heavyweight title
fights, dazzling, dressed-to-kill is the for
From Jack Johnson thru Joe Lou
blacks were relegated to the bleac
nigger-heaven balconies.
But Ali brought them
to ringside to pay homage.
So enter the peacocks,
an expression of black
pride. Colorful, flam
boyant, spectacular,
these exotic fashion
plates first turned
out in style, en masse,
at the Ali-Quarry
bout in Atlanta "71.
Sequined hot pants,
leathers, mink midi-coats,
capes, velvets. Out going,
bright, arrogant, happy.
The trend reached it's
crescendo at the first Al
Frazier fight at Madison Square Gard

LeRoy Neiman

New York Hotel
fight nite
March 8, '71

Johnny T.
Tap Dancer J. Crutch...

Blacks Blackein' it
Regency Hotel lobby
fight nite Oct 26 '70
LeRoy Neiman
Atlanta

March 8 '71
fight nite
Mad. Sq. Garden
N.Y.
LeRoy Neiman

Pink Dude

New York
LeRoy Neiman

ROUND III

ROUND IV

Joe Frazier

LeRoy Neiman

Round 15
Frazier-Ali
Madison Sq. Garden 3-8-71

March 8, 1971...Ali and Frazier, heroic figures, both somewhat defeated by the fight...embarrassed by their uncharacteristic wounds, neither wanted to be seen ...their bruises were grotesque, as though they had been in a wreck, not a prize fight...when Ali went down, the ring shrank...little did he realize how he resembled the Greek sculpture of the fallen Gaul.

149

LeRoy Neiman '71

Ringside at a big fight unites the reigning powers of the underworld and social register...with a good array of front-row-burlesque bald heads and expensive blondes... you never see a bad set of legs in the first row...with the ascent of Ali, the black man *integrated* the ringside seats...boxing is only real up close...the old champions are introduced in the ring, as if to prove they are fit and alive and have survived...to view a fight on television is like looking at the reproduction of a painting...the true aficionado even watches the prelims, where the fighters going up and those coming down meet halfway...he also finds it important to experience the gym, so squalid, sweaty, dreary...much like the ballet rehearsal room...but here is beauty, too...the aged and out-of-shape work the corners...the cut man, companion, pail carrier ...and the success-softened, alligator-shod fight manager...after climbing the ring steps for 10 rounds, they're more tired than the fighters...the doctor at ringside is the enemy of the crowd... at any moment he might interrupt the bloodbath...audience disapproval is balanced by a percentage of fans who are pleased when the doctor stops the proceeding—if that's where their money is.

151

er and Yank Durham
after Ali fight
Madison Square Garden 3-8-71
Neiman
The Winner!

153

*gliding, supple, lithe, agile,
capering, graceful, bounding, enigmatic,
Born Louisville Ky.*

Harliquin
Born Bergamo, Italy

cupidity,
catapulting,
volitile,

paradoxical rascality,
Exciting elusive

Harlequin is one of the most mysterious figures ever
created. Over his four centuries he has always changed
with the times.

Harlequin

Dali has the hands of a peasant, fine delicate
facial structure of an aristocrat, and a great ear.
a gentle religious man he says the heart is the church in every man.

Dali

LeRoy Neiman
April 7 '72
New York

LeRoy Neiman
Malibu '66

Larger than Life

The Wehrmacht helmets with the swastika emblazoned on the side, favored by California surfers in the '60s, somehow failed to catch on...possibly for the same reason the Hitler mustache never could have made it in the pop culture.

In London at Sotheby and Co., founded 1774, time and tradition are allies of auctioneer Peter Wilson, who occupies the last working throne of England...and speaks with more authority from his—to the art world—than the Queen does to the Commonwealth from her royal seat.

Now we have a
painting by Gustave
Moreau — The property of
la Baronne Elie de Rothschild, of Paris
"Venus sortant de l'Onde"
Start at — 2000 pounds — 4,000
5, 6, 7 thousand, 8, 9, 10, 11, 12, 13, 14
15, 15 thousand, 16, 17, 19, 20, 21, 22,
22 thousand pounds on my right,
sold for 22,000 £'s
It is yours Sir

ST.

Sotheby & Co.
34-35 New Bond St.
London W.1.

Peter Wilson
Auction
Wed. 21st April 1971
LeRoy Neiman

buyers at Sotheby sale
21 April '71
LeRoy Neiman

159

no apparent decline in dignity or finances…after buffing a mirror finish on Frank Sinatra's shoes in his Fontainebleau Hotel sub-lobby concession, he announced proudly: "It's an honor to shine the leather of Mr. Sinatra—he's the greatest" …later, in his suite, I detected the same pride in Frank's voice as he told me: "I'll have you know the kicks I'm wearing are shined daily by Beau Jack, one of the greatest welters who ever threw leather."

Dec 2 '72   President Nixon
Henry A. Kessinger ADVISER ON national affairs

Public figures are always conscious of their extremities…hand-in-pocket is an acceptable vulgarity of a gentleman's posture…the President of the United States and his then adviser on foreign affairs are frequently photographed in that attitude…an affectation common to Washington, where pressure drives men to small gestures.

In the army the dog rubber generally commanded more respect than the chaplain's assistant…in the tourist mecca of Miami Beach, Beau Jack has elevated the role of shining shoes to the level of his crowd-pleasing days as a Madison Square Garden headliner…with

160

Beau Jack
shining Sinatra's Shoes
Fontainebleau Miami Beach
LeRoy Neiman 4-8-67

Sexy at 81, living proof that you don't have to smoke or drink to have a good time. Mae West, monument to health food and clean habits, 20-20 vision - All senses ALERT.

Margaret Mead was one of the few people I sketched who, at age 70, exuded potential...Dr. Mead didn't confine her investigation to civilized society....The underdog in society is important...the protestor in Watts attempted to establish his own identity...and three young Puerto Rican reinsmen found celebrity and security riding thoroughbreds, and added their own zest and flash to the already colorful silk room....In 1959, as Maurice Chevalier approached 70, I accompanied him to the stage of the Empire Room in Chicago's Palmer House, easing his burden by carrying his straw hat.

Carlos Lopez   Eddie Belmonte   Angel Cordero Jr.

LeRoy Neiman '71

There was an attitude about De Gaulle at the height of his power that simply resurrected the Napoleonic influence.

Napoleon commissioned artists to document his every gesture — created the art salon. In 1803 an English heavyweight Jem Belcher was called "the Napoleon of the Ring"

"Scarface" Al Capone — first public enemy No 1. Veteran of W.W. 1

Founder of the first soup kitchen

To paint figures of past historical prominence...Napoleon, De Gaulle, Capone, Behan...is like preparing a police drawing from photographs, interviews and the memories of others....Great leaders are often great users or champions of art...Lincoln sat repeatedly for early photographers and Teddy Roosevelt was confirmed as a national hero by Frederic Remington's painting of the charge up San Juan Hill. The great military feats of Napoleon led to many decades of heroic French battlefield paintings....I never sketch a moment of pro football action without recalling the grand hall of battle paintings at Versailles ...like our weekly pro gridiron spectacles, the battle of Waterloo took place on a Sunday.

In the far corner of the
lobby near the bar
Brendan Behan (POSTHUMOUSLY)
at the Algonquin
W 44 St.
New York

LeRoy Neiman '70

George Chuvalo
Canadian Heavyweight Champion

LeRoy Neiman '68

Our talk-show society has encouraged today's actors and athletes to be taken seriously…submitting their views on a wide range of subjects beyond the fields of their own excellence…it is sometimes difficult to lend the proper attention to someone plumbing his own depths when one is confronted by, say, a prize fighter's ring-scarred face, its features moved and relocated by human fists….Tough guys can be charitable…during the Kefauver hearings in the early 1950s, the TV cameras could show only the hands of the key witness, Frank Costello…an English Oval cigarette dangled constantly between his manicured fingers…in gratitude for the publicity, the cigarette manufacturer sent the "man in gray" continuous supplies of their product, which he in turn donated to VA hospitals….Most physically tough guys neglect their bodies in middle age and run to fat…but it never concerns them because they can still settle issues the same old way…the knuckle sandwich.

FRANK Costello
Ringside Torres Tiger
Madison Square Garden
Dec 16. 66

Irish pub regulars sing and brawl the same as they did in Joyce's Dublin when they have their jar.

LeRoy Neiman
Dublin '64

167

Dr. Armand Hammer
Chairman of the Board
Hammer Galleries   Knoedler Galleries
Occidental Petroleum Co.   LeRoy Neiman
Armand Hammer   8-27, '73 New Yo

Tough diplomacy, not muscle, is the language of the international art dealer — you never mistake the firmness of this guy on the telephone. It isn't necessary to see him. Art is all, but Dr. Hammer's duty to his collectors and stockholders is foremost.

One of the original
beautiful people —
Summer of '62
Acting the part of the
Mediterranean Swashbuckler.

7-12-'62

Sean Flynn
San Remo

Trinity Church
74 Trinity St. NY
Wall St.
LeRoy Neiman

the Men in grey

In the context of the social problems of the '70s, the habitués of Forty-deuce Street and the Bowery have become somewhat more acceptable...in certain ways they reflect the higher community ethics...they go to church, don't demonstrate, are nonviolent, are among the first to recycle waste products, and when they solicit funds you can be confident the money won't be invested in drugs ...the true wino never flaunts his appreciation of the grape, and modestly conceals his bottle of Gypsy Rose in a paper bag...they dress in colors of quiet taste: muted, well-related grays...they have adjusted to their environment.

Bowery N.Y.   *LeRoy Neiman*

Le Rouge ou
Le Noir

Liverpool
Grand National
Antree England
26th March 1960
LeRoy Neiman

I think in words when I paint...
the big wheel...the hazard table
...the carpeted casino...the gaming room...from the ticker tapes
of Wall Street to the green felt spas
of Las Vegas, the high rollers are
drawn to the *temple de la chance*
...the New York Stock Exchange
is a kind of cavernous casino...
the 12 trading posts, horseshoe-
shaped in the center of the floor,
are like crap tables...and the
booths on the fringe of the room
suggest the slots...age and station
are of no concern to the betting
gentry...the good Irish priest
crosses the Irish Sea to bet on the
nags at Liverpool...a first com-
municant, age 7 or 8, acts as a
runner for the bookmaker at a
Dublin dog track...and places
bets for his parents, neighborhood
idlers...and himself.

Monte Carlo
'70
LeRoy Neiman

casino Dubrovnik
Yugoslavia
LeRoy Neiman
'67

Harolds Cross
greyhound Track
5-15-70 Dublin

Belmont
Race Track
Paddock Dining Room
May 30 '73
LeRoy Neiman

173

Scrooge

LeRoy Neiman

J. Paul Getty
4-5-61   London

Rich Guys

The artist who experiences success finds himself dealing with men of power and fortune....."The truly rich," J. Paul Getty once assured me, "can afford to owe vast sums of money."...Over a lifetime dedicated to amassing great wealth, features contract and pinch...by a mean age of 75 these corporate giants all tend to look alike...resembling the hawklike visage of Scrooge, who stands for thrift, or Uncle Sam, who doesn't.

Uncle Sam   John D. Rockefeller

John D. knew Uncle Sam from the good old days of Capt. Jonathan, EN. 1861, and Brother Jonathan, 1875

Les Femmes

In feminine beauty the bone surfaces in just the right places…no matter how voluptuous, you can always touch the bone, if necessary through a dimple…a woman of timeless beauty commands the situation she is in…backed up by aesthetic scenery or not, gowned or unclothed, her beauty holds in the same way that a great painting can hang anywhere, or be thrown into the corner of an artist's loft… and lose none of its quality and dignity…beauty is infinite in its variety….In today's Morocco a nude ankle in a sidewalk café is as exciting as in 19th century Victorian England…the tattoos and gold teeth that were once considered signs of beauty have been discarded by Moroccan women…but the coquettish veil of mystery hasn't disappeared…to that traditional fashion has been added the modern touch of shades and styl-

Les Baigneuses

Jean Shrimpton
Sunday Nov 16 '69
Lake Geneva
LeRoy Neiman

Rabat Moroco *LeRoy Neiman '69*

ARIANE ANASTASSOPOULOS
Club Méditerranée *AGADIR MOROCCO*
JULY 27 '69 *LeRoy Neiman*

ish footwear....A stunning Greek jet-setter typifies the beauty who has a passport to the world...she knows the rules...has been to the right schools...speaks any language...is equally at home at Saint-Tropez, Acapulco, Palm Beach, Deauville, Sardinia...she is perfectly aimed...she's on time ...she's now.

In the paddock of any racetrack in the world, the fashionable female stable owners and mistresses of stud farms are commanding figures...the aristocratic woman at sport....Fashion models who gravitate to Paris from anywhere, Oriental, black or Latin, all become exclusively Parisienne, with the chic, gamin look that shapes their entire being....Jean Shrimpton made parting her hair to eat an elegant gesture....Russian peasant women have been liberated for centuries...that is, doing man's work ...they present dark silhouettes, the somber utility of their dress accented by the color of their babushkas...formidable.

LeRoy Neiman

Samburu Kenya
Aug. 6, '70

李真衣子　リーまいこ

those modern Japanese beauties who have not surrendered
to the plastic surgeon's scalpel, seeking the western look,
retain the traditional outline of brow and cheek,
narrow eyes, half parted petal lips and graceful, delica

Maiko Lee

hands. These exquisite creatures, still precious and extravagant in appearance, are masters of artifice and betoken hours before the mirror, totally absorbed in the task of maintaining their beauty.

One type of American working girl, the Times Square courtesan whose office is the sidewalk, creates her own orbit...with a cast of satellites—the pimp, cop and client —constantly circling around her. ...In the black-is-beautiful era, black women are knockouts...on safari I sketched African tribal women in Samburu and Serengetti ...real lookers who spared nothing in the effort to recruit the attention of the male members by ornamenting themselves...it appeared that the more she decorated herself, the

184

Sugar

42
St.

Peaches

Butter

Delancy & Kenmare
N.Y.C. LeRoy Neiman '74

Restaurant
Maisons-Lafitte
Race Course

Mr and
Mme André Bollack
April 27 71

STRAWBERRY
Blonde

Beverly Sills
Rehearsal for Anna
Bolena
9-29-73
LeRoy Neiman

Kremlin   LeRoy Neiman
                 '65

Gina Byram
1st Bunny of the Year
LeRoy Neiman

more she announced her availability...the inventiveness of her African sisters has passed to today's black beauty, presenting her as the freshest and most exciting female on the American girlwatching scene..."the darker the berry, the sweeter the juice."

In the chronology of irresistible ladies, today's counterpart of the Ziegfeld girl is the Playboy bunny, the first redesigned women in decades....In the salon of art and cheesecake, the Gibson Girl, the John Held flapper and the Petty Girl form a vanity line that led to the Femlin—a combination of *feminine* and *gremlin*—my own creation, who has occupied a corner of my brain...and the party-joke page of *Playboy*...for the past 20 years.

187

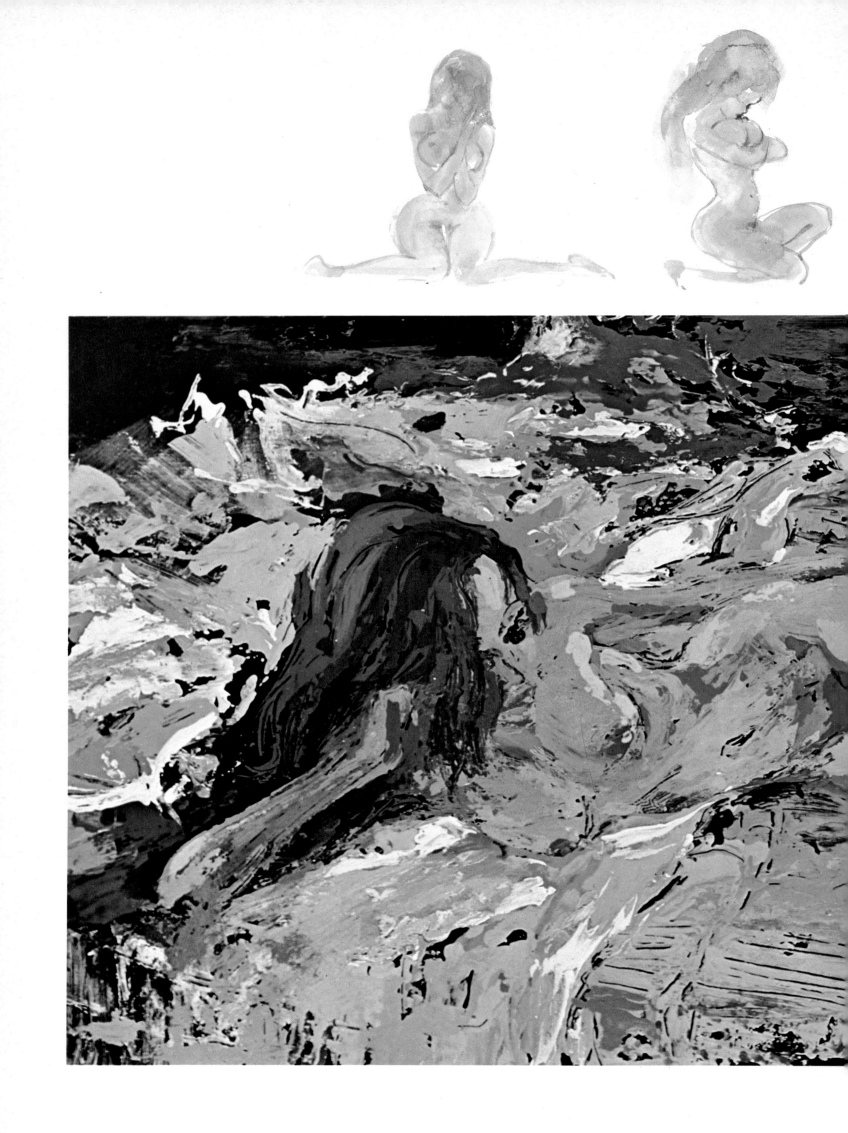

Playboyland

In the salad days of *Playboy*, starting in 1954, the challenge was quality...for me the artistic experience was exploring social situations, sketching in public, exposing one's talent to the curious and disinterested at play, or performing their affluent distractions...20 years later the challenge is somewhat different....I am one of the people I was looking at...now I must look out, from within....Although sex sold the magazine and gave it notoriety, on a more subtle level understood at first by only a few, Hugh Hefner was elevating the magazine's tone by offering a new outlet for creative expression to writers, artists and humorists.... *Playboy* gave me leave to roam the haut monde, and carte blanche to check out the sporting life milieu. ...While building the *Playboy* empire, Hef established the Chicago mansion as a refuge for the rich in talent . . . intellectual stimulation came from a continuing mixture of actors, writers, comics, politicians, clergymen and playmates—a cross section of American fantasy.

Mort Sahl
1340 N. State
Chicago
July 20 '63

Sharon Rogers
Bobbie Arnstien

Hef

Shel Silverstein

In the '60s I was hung up on sketching nudes as landscapes, which amounted to a gal on a mussed-up bed . . . a bedscape . . . the *Playboy* mansion provided an inexhaustible supply of material. . . . I only regret that because of the warmth of the friendships that invariably resulted, I always felt obligated to give the drawings to the subject . . . on request.

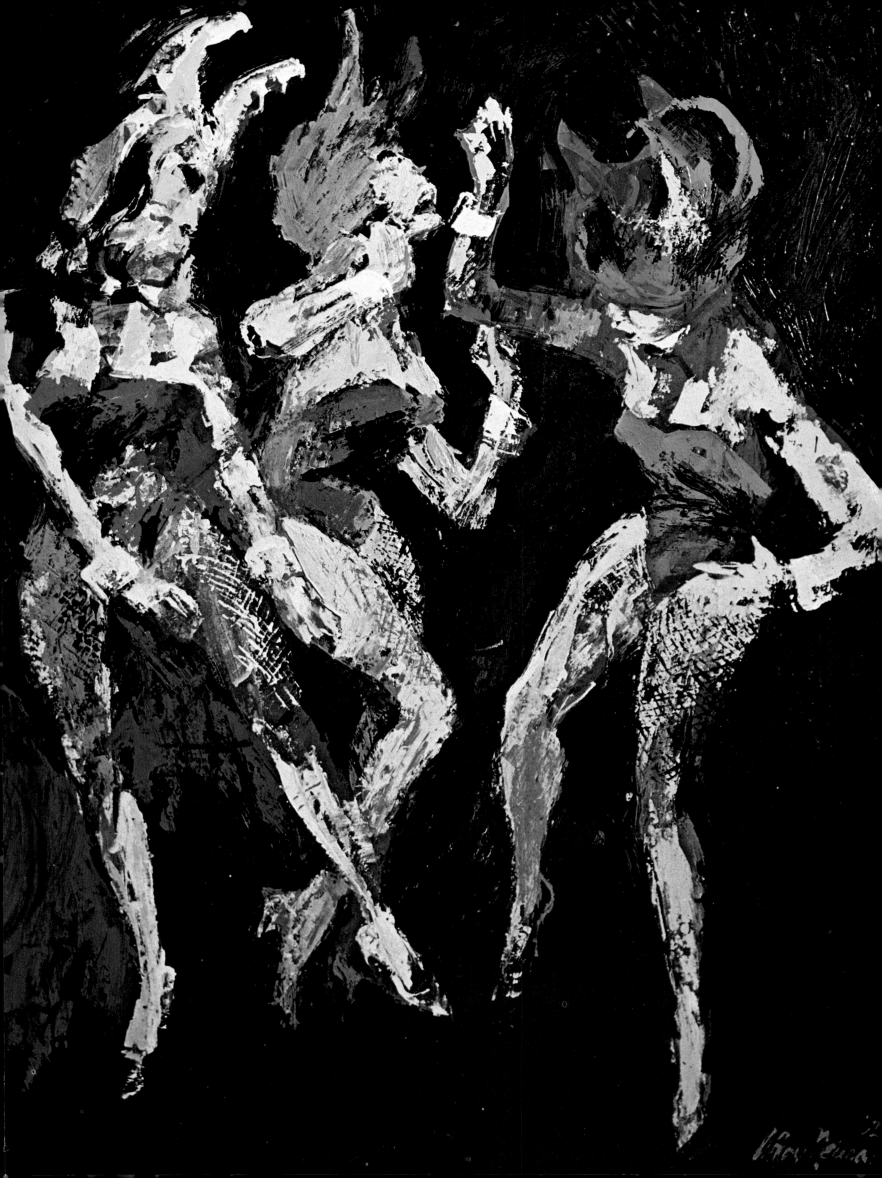

NINO BENVENUTI

MADISON SQUARE GARDEN
MONDAY, APRIL 17, 1967
PRESS INFORMATION

NAME OF BOXER   WHERE FROM   TRUNKS   WEIGHT
----
15 ROUNDS -- MAIN EVENT -- 15 ROUNDS
EMILE GRIFFITH   NEW YORK CITY   WHITE   153 1/2
NINO BENVENUTI   TRIESTE, ITALY   RED   159

Benvenuti after his victory

LeRoy Neiman
4-7-67

Reclining Figures

It is impossible to pass through a normal day without encountering a reclining figure...we start each day as a reclining figure...and you may find yourself next to one upon awakening...it could be a figure at rest before an activity, or exhausted after...sometimes during, as a Bowery bum catching a quick nap before the cops rap the soles of his shoes...or a chilled fighter flatter than a piece of gold leaf, taking a

Madison Ave chicago
LeRoy Neiman ...'54

Q.B. Joe
Before Houston Jet Game
N Oct. 10, '68

LeRoy Neiman
Shea Stadium N.Y.

Cleveland Williams.
"Big Cat" K.O.'d by Ali
Astrodome Houston.
Nov. 14, '66

LeRoy Neiman '70

197

Sweet Sweat

Central Park
N.Y.

LeRoy Neiman
'73

I carry in my sketchbook at all times an assortment of different numbered drawing and fountain pens...sharp and clean, pen and ink is ideal to capture the positive and negative...nothing challenges the eye and hand more than the movement, rhythm and emotion of Afro-Americans dancing well... when you draw something fluid, to music, it actually influences the tempo at which you work...every limber, unerasable line is a mark of the beat as the bodies of Chocolate Darlings and their Bad Dudes bend, rock, jive, jam, burn, sway or dance tight...grooving.

199

Hockey

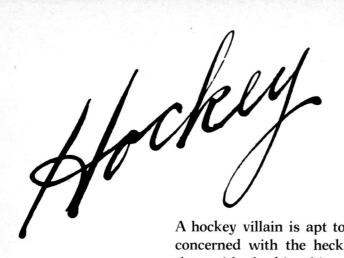

A hockey villain is apt to be less concerned with the heckling fan than with checking his reflection in the glass as he glides along the boards...the sport's speed is accentuated by the long, mod hair of many players, which flows straight back as they streak past, making them appear swifter than they are...like Mercury...the iceman is covered with nearly as many numbers (9) on his uniform and gear as a businessman's well-labeled attire (15-plus) when suited up for winter action.

march 16, '73 Boucha – Sanderson
N.B.C. T.V.
DETROIT Olympia
LeRoy Neiman

LeRoy Neiman
Detroit Olympia 3-16-73

Wayne Cashman

Gilbert
Ratelle

N.Y. Rangers
Madison Square Garden '73

Madison Sq. Garden   Chicago Blackhawks '69

203

World's Pocket Billiard Championship
champion Luther Lassiter vs. Challenger
Art Cranfield
Palm Garden New York City Sept 24 '64
LeRoy Neiman

Black tie Billiards

A certain level of skill in billiards was once regarded as evidence of a misspent youth...from pool-hall hustler to tuxedoed tournament player, our hero is the same guy ...to wear the tux in billiards one must move through the ranks... an important match requires the proper dramatic setting...armed with their cues, the players enter the ballroom and step over the rope, which marks off the playing area, onto the red carpet...they present elegant shapes, silhouettes in black, as they circle the table with a surgeon's assurance.

Yankee Stadium

LeRoy Neiman

Oct. 1 1963

Sandy Koufax, striking out
Mickey Mantle
1ST Game 1963 World Series
Koufax fans 15

LeRoy Neiman
Hank Aaron

Baseball

Ballparks in today's renovated cities are like churches in medieval villages...these round, white structures represent sort of the core of the inner city...the baseball player is a working man in the context of sports...his season—from spring training to play-offs—can cover up to 215 days out of the year...the average working chap, with time off for holidays, is at his job 230 days... like any other working or professional man, the successful ballplayer fails two out of three times at bat...the baseball manager looks young on the field, secure in the looseness of his uniform, but up close looks older than his years ...in a tight game there is a hush in the park between the time the ball leaves the pitcher's hand and arrives at the plate.

210

N.Y. Met Rusty Staub
Dodger dugout
Dodger Stadium
L.A.
LeRoy Neiman
6 P.M.
73
autograph session

Roberto
Clementi

Willie
Stargel

Johnny
Bench

Dick Allen

Estadio Polideportivo Maracaibo   17 Marzo 1971

N.Y. Yankee Dugout

"Yogi"
Ft. Lauderdale
Stadium
Florida
March 2 '64

LeRoy Neiman

Dick Williams   Sparky Anderson   Chuck Tanner

Leo and the Mets

OAKLAND STY'S MM'N
METS R MY PETS

Vida Blue.
World Series
5th game Shea Stadium
Mets 2 A's 0
Oct 18th '73
LeRoy Neiman

The dugout is the last of the true men's clubs...private, profane, with spitting on the floor encouraged...nobody spits as often, or as expressively, as the baseball player...he writes best on the curve, from signing so many baseballs...no other vantage point in sports offers a more close-up feeling of danger than next to the batting cage...you see the batter uncoil and the vibration of the bat in his hand as he connects...or feel the force of the ball as it strikes the screen in front of you...once the game begins, the umpire behind the plate has the location the artist would choose—closest to the action...like a kid in the front row at the movies.

212

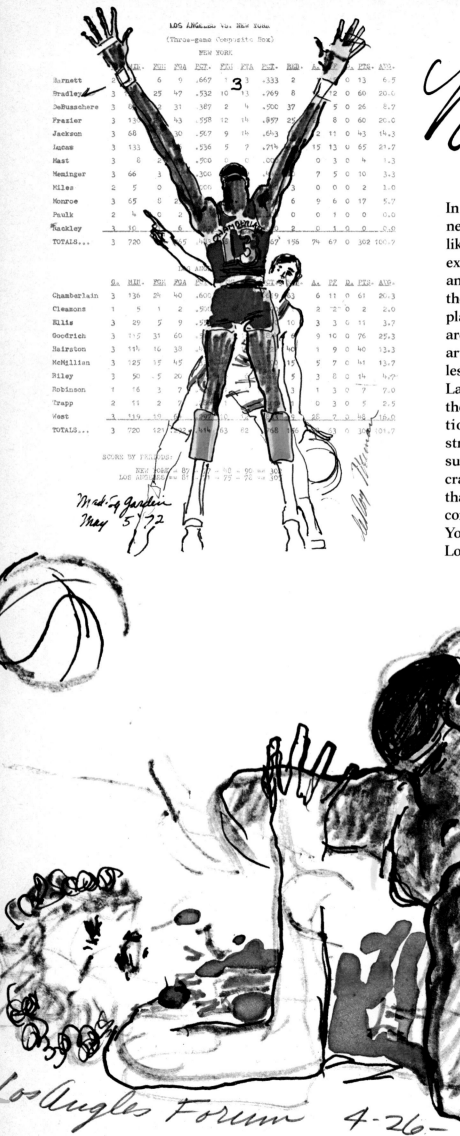

LOS ANGELES VS. NEW YORK
(Three-game Composite Box)

NEW YORK

	G.	MIN.	FGM	FGA	PCT.	FTM	FTA	PCT.	REB.	A.	PF	D.	PTS.	AVG.
Barnett	2		6	9	.667		3	.333	2			0	13	6.5
Bradley	3		25	47	.532	10	13	.769	8		12	0	60	20.0
DeBusschere	3	8		31	.387	2	4	.500	37		5	0	26	8.7
Frazier	3	13		43	.558	12	14	.857	25		8	0	60	20.0
Jackson	3	68		30	.567	9	14	.643	2	11		0	43	14.3
Lucas	3	133			.536	5	7	.714	15	13		0	65	21.7
Mast	3	8			.500	0	0	.00	0	3		4	1.3
Meminger	3	66	3		.300				7	5		0	10	3.3
Miles	2	5	0		.000				0	0		0	2	1.0
Monroe	3	65	8						6	9	6	0	17	5.7
Paulk	2	4	0						0	0		0	0	0.0
Rackley	3	10	6						2	0	1	0	0	0.0
TOTALS...	3	720			.482		67	156	74	67	0	302	100.7

LOS ANGELES

	G.	MIN.	FGM	FGA	PCT.	FTM	FTA	PCT.	REB.	A.	PF	D.	PTS.	AVG.
Chamberlain	3	136	24	40	.600				63	6	11	0	61	20.3
Cleamons	1	5	1	2	.500				2	2	0	0	2	2.0
Ellis	3	29	5	9	.55				10	3	3	0	11	3.7
Goodrich	3	115	31	60					9	10	0	76	25.3
Hairston	3	114	16	38					40	1	9	0	40	13.3
McMillian	3	125	15	45					15	5	7	0	41	13.7
Riley	3	50	5	20					5	3	8	0	14	4.7
Robinson	1	16	3	7					1	3	0	7	7.0
Trapp	2	11	2	7					0	3	0	5	2.5
West	3	119	19		.397	10			28	7	0	48	16.0
TOTALS...	3	720	121		.414	63	82	.768	156		63	0	306	101.7

SCORE BY PERIODS:

NEW YORK = 87 - 40 - 90 == 302
LOS ANGELES == 81 - 75 - 78 = 306

Madison Garden
May 5/72

In all of sports, basketball is the nearest to pop art...the mirror-like finish of the floor, with its exotic, colorful symbols...the cut and markings of the uniforms... the shape of the baskets...and the playgrounds where backboards are covered with graffiti, the pop art of the underground....Regardless of record, the Knicks and the Lakers are the glamour teams of the pros...in my art I use elongation to exaggerate...but why stretch the point with these lanky supergiants?...The sight of them crashing to the floor is almost more than the eye, or the sketchpad, can contain...first they tower like New York high-rises, then sprawl like Los Angeles.

Los Angeles Forum *4-26-72*

Jack Nicklaus
Doral
Country Club
Florida
'73

Pairings and Starting Time

Jack and Arnie

Once, at the Westchester Classic, a loose page blew out of my sketch-pad and fluttered toward Jack Nicklaus as he lined up a shot...his partner, Doug Sanders, arrested the paper in flight with his driver and pinned it to the ground ...concentrating totally, Jack never noticed...I spent a wet A.M. with Arnold Palmer on the practice tee at the Masters in '73...his army followed us under their Arnold Palmer umbrellas....I sketched him cutting the rain, soaked... while I could perform my art under shelter, Arnie couldn't.

217

Weathermen

The high-priced star enjoys no favor on the field. He endures the same hardships of weather the fans do...from the 100-plus heat of a pre-season night in the south ...to the brain-freezing cold of a 15-above day in December...or a rain-and-sleet chilled November afternoon at Shea Stadium.... Football is the only sport where, legitimately, 50 people can be on the field at one time (44 players and six officials), as the teams change sides....When, at the age of 24, Stephen Crane wrote *The Red Badge of Courage*, he had never seen combat...unable to gain a perspective of war from the vantage of an ordinary, unromantic soldier, he drew his insights by recalling the fierce physical combat he had experienced on the college football field....From my vantage point along the sidelines the hawkish fans—many having forsaken church for stadium services—seem engaged in a holy war ...at my back comes a vibrating barrage of vocal artillery fire... from the other side of the stadium the enemy returns the fire...while on the battlefield the infantry collide head-on, making the earth tremble...in the middle of this madness, sketching can become a shaky proposition.

N.Y. Jets–Denver
Shea Stadium
Oct. 13, '61

LeRoy Neiman

"Bot ears"
Number 12
Shea stadium

219

LeRoy Neiman '69

Nobis   Van Brocklin
New Orleans Saints - Atlanta Falcons
10-25-70   Atlanta Stadium
                    LeRoy Neiman

...iker warming up

Space heater
Electricity and Karosine
LeRoy Neiman

Kicker
O'Neil

221

K.C. game Dec. 14.
Shea   '73

Half Time
Shea Stadium
Nov. 10 '68
LeRoy Neiman

224

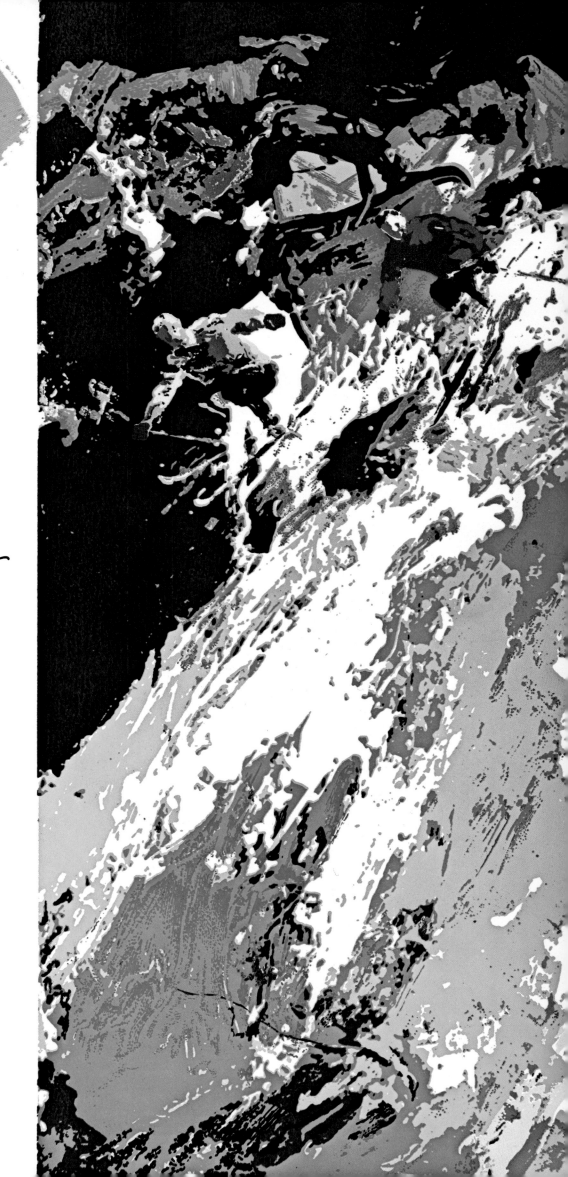

Downers

In the international play scene, the only thing more glamorous than an Argentine polo player is a Peruvian skier, with his tinted eye shields....Female skiers, in their adhesive stretch pants, contribute measurably to the aesthetics of the sport....The recreational skier has urbanized the slopes...natives living at the foot of the mountains who have never skied or climbed them are nonetheless authorities on the perils and glories that exist there...they speak critically and give advice readily about the condition of the mountain, though they have never experienced it... their opinions are important to the chapstick set and cannot be ignored...I relate this to the art critic and the artist.

Wladyslaw Komar
Sept. '72 Polen

München 〇〇〇 10.9.1972 15.30 h

Cérémonie de Clôture
et Prix des Nations
Closing Ceremony
and Olympic Jumping
Grand Prix
Schlußfeier und
Preis der Nationen

Olympiastadion

press

Bloc
Block   Y³

Rang
Row   54
Reihe

Place
Seat
Platz

01753

XX th Olympiad

MUNICH, West Germany, September 1972—here 200 gold-medal winners (and 10,000 losers) pursued the Olympic motto: *citius, altius, fortius*—swifter, higher, stronger...the excitement began to pyramid from the moment the teams of 126 nations paraded into Munich's acrylic-domed stadium, sweeping past the grandstands in a panoply of color...from the vividly costumed Mexicans to the proud Japanese and the formidable Mongolians...as massed bands played folk melodies rather than the martial anthems of other years ...there was joy and communication as the small, smartly dressed

XX Olympiad
Aug 25 72   Münich   Running towards the
LeRoy Neiman   Olympiastadion

XXth Olympiad   München
Ringer-Judo Halle
Museogelände
LeRoy Neiman   '72

110 5'11" Rod Milburn Jr. 110 M Hurdles

Frei Aug 21 '72

Milburn Training running barefoot on the grass with Mania Rodlin

Olga Korbut

Practice

Sporthalle Olympiapark

Mark Spitz Aug. 31, '72 UNTER DER TROCKEN HAUBE

*Wassili Alexejew
XX Olympiad* — *Gewichtheberhalle
Messegelände* — *LeRoy Neiman
Munich Sept. 1, '72*

LeRoy Neiman — *Schwimmhalle*

Israeli team marched into the stadium to receive one of the day's largest ovations...from the circus-tented coliseum to the modern dormitories, there was a powerful quality about the architecture of all the buildings...but in the midst of vast technology, it was the athletes who counted...there was drama and contrast wherever one looked ...the weightlifters trained constantly and thought of little else but improving their strength... Russia's porcelain doll, Olga Korbut, 88 pounds of charm, turned tears into cheers with her audacious gymnastic style...one could enjoy the finesse of the fencers...the ballet tumbling of the gymnasts...the exaggerated motion of the heel-and-toe walkers ...the drama at the Schwimhalle was the most exhausting, as I sketched Mark Spitz winning medal after gold medal, until he made his seven...what a natural!

229

Olympic Park Sept 6 '72
München   LeRoy Neiman

Danmark Handball Team
playing improvised interteam game
called Foot-Tennis on volleyball
court with net lowered. —wing
Handball

LeRoy Neiman

Wrestling and Judo Hall Messegelände

Games of the XXth Olympics
Munich Aug. 26 '72

Munich XX Olympiad
Aug. 26, '72

Opening Ceremony
Entry march of Israeli team *Olympic Stadium – Olympic Park*
LeRoy Neiman *August 26 '72* *Munich*

...The camaraderie, the festive mood, infected the village as athletes from around the world reached out to each other...traded pins and mementoes...competed at such non-Olympic sports as chess, pinball and one-hole golf ...and forgot their national chauvinisms in the discothèque, where the beauty and the beef of the XXth Olympiad gathered nightly... where rhythmic Africans danced to American rock...and athletes of different cultures met, played, visited, became advanced beyond the hand-holding stage...movement, always, everywhere...in that place, at that time, it was impossible not to believe in the Olympic ideals and spirit.

232

LeRoy Neiman *Korean Soccer Players play Soccer Game*
Recreation Center – Olympic Village *Aug. 23 '7*

XX Olympiad
Olympic Village
Aug. 25 '72   München   LeRoy Neiman

Club Bavarian
Olympic Village
München   LeRoy Neiman
Sept. 1 '72

IZEI

POLI

POLIZEI

München Sept.

Sadly, the dominant memory for all would not be the joy of the Games, but the tragic, near endless day of September 5...the sun shone brilliantly, but never was a mood darker or gloomier...the buildings of the village—which were designed around a central play area, the scene of so many friendly international exchanges— suddenly took on the look of a hopeless penitentiary...the hordes of armed police, the truckloads of military and, always, the eternal eye of the TV cameras panning and pointing...the atmosphere grew more oppressive as the tanks rolled in, the sky darkened, the final floodlit carnage drew near.

POLIZEI

P.M.
72

Olympic Village

LeRoy Neiman

Russia

From the window of my room in the National Hotel (where once Lenin stayed), I sketched the funeral of Yuri Gagarin, the Soviet space hero.... As the procession solemnly crossed Revolution Square and marched into Red Square, the changes of light and color on Red Square were deep and rich with beauty...St. Basil's, with its onion-topped turrets, looming majestic at the top of the Square.

St. Basil
Cathedral
March 28, '68
LeRoy Neiman

Ballet is not so much an art as a way of life...its dancers are honored members of the Russian elite. After a performance, balletomanes take control. A handful of frenzied handclappers can detain the lead dancers for repeated curtain calls long after the audience has filed out.

238

LeRoy Neiman, Bolshoi '68, Swan Lake, Palace of Congresses, Kremlin

Bolshoi Theatre   Wed. March 27 1968

Funeral Procession
of Yuri Gagarin '68

Big Money Chess!

REYKJAVIK, September 1972— Bobby Fischer leaves his hotel with all the adulation and adoration that accompanies a matador leaving the Palace Hotel in Madrid... his fans are the children and ladies of Iceland, blond and blue-eyed ...his own appearance, disheveled, mussed, more closely resembles that of a man leaving a police station after an all-night grilling

Boris Spassky U.S.S.R.

next year
"BA HA SHANNA HA

...his mind is elsewhere...he has the manner of a prize fighter on his way to the arena, except without fear...Fischer is the first chess player with that contemporary, sports-star attitude...when he thrusts his right hand forward to make a sudden move, it is the motion of a fighter delivering a hard, jarring punch...I can almost see Spassky with a bloodied nose.

Bobby Fischer
USA

Bobby Fisher leaving
Loftleidir Hotel for match,
Reykjavik Iceland

July '72 LeRoy Neiman

B. Spassky   R. Fischer
July 27 '72
World's Chess Championship
Reykjavik, Iceland.

LeRoy Neiman

Fischer-Spassky world
Chess Champion-
Reykjavik, Iceland ship
Bobby Fischer with his
13 yr old - playing 4 year

LeRoy Neiman

Gudlaug Porsteinsd
11 year old

July 29 72   LeRoy Neiman

Miguel Najdorf

Utgardur/Glassbar
Fédération Islandaise des Echecs
30-30 Tournament   July 29 72
Reykjavik, Iceland.

Fischer
Reykjavik, Iceland   July 27, '72

Louis
Armstrong

Olympia
Paris '61

Satch
Chez Paree, Chicago. *LeRoy Neiman* '56

Satchmo

I crossed paths often with Louis Armstrong . . . sketched and painted him countless times from Chicago to New York to Paris... Satchmo singing or blowing, the familiar white handkerchief as an accent....At my one-man show at Hammer Gallery in New York, in 1963, he bought a painting of Gerry Mulligan and paid me a compliment I'll always treasure: "Pops, you've painted a few"...I sketched him last with Duke Ellington, the two giants of jazz...he looked tired, spent and beautiful...he died not long after.

Mad. Sq. Garden N.Y.   2-23-70   *LOUIS and Duke*
LeRoy Neiman

Frank

To be with Frank Sinatra is to be in the company of an artist...I think of him not only as a singer but as a musician...his conversation is textured with musical terms...he lives to perform, and even in retirement seemed to be marking time between music...I find him a man of sentiment who, in his own way, loves art...he once shyly told me of a painting he had done of the New York skyline at night, from Hoboken, just across the river...many a wooing session has advanced to the songs of Sinatra, softly, in the background...on car radios or record players...in the front seat with the top down or on the porch swing or a picnic blanket ...three generations of young lovers owe him a debt.

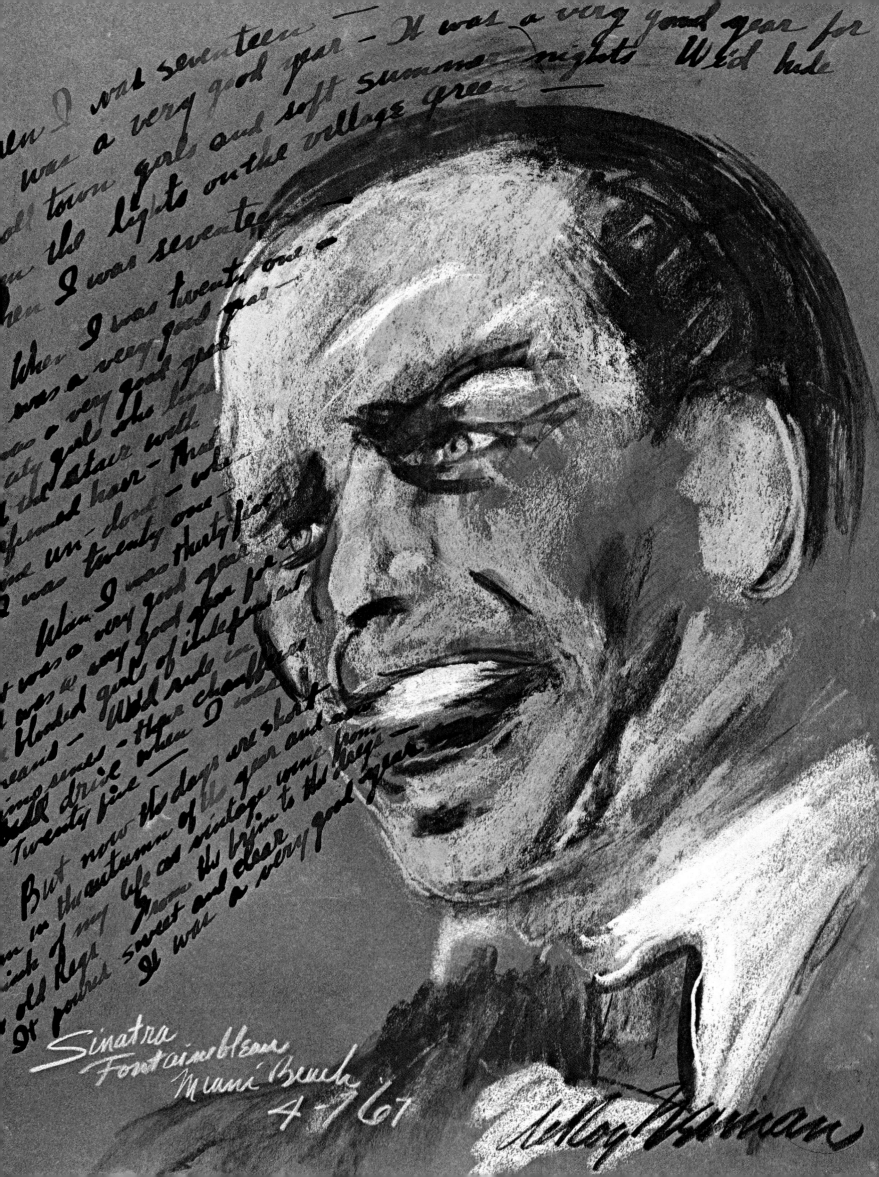

When I was seventeen —
— It was a very good year — It was a very good year for
all town girls and soft summer nights We'd hide
on the lights on the village green —
When I was seventeen —

When I was twenty one —
— was a very good year —
city girls who lived
up the stair with
perfumed hair — that
came un — don't — one
— was twenty one —

When I was thirty five
— It was a very good year —
It was a very good year for
blooded girls of independent
means — We'd ride in
limousines — their chauffeurs
Twenty five when I would drive —

But now the days are short
— I'm in the autumn of the year and now
I think of my life as vintage wine from
fine old kegs — from the brim to the dregs —
It poured sweet and clear — It was a very good year

Sinatra
Fontainebleau
Miami Beach
4-7-67
LeRoy Neiman

Duke Elling

Jack Dempsey

Look Alikes

Little did Jack Dempsey realize when he attended the funeral of his contemporary Duke Ellington at the Cathedral of St. John the Divine on May 27, 1974 in New York that they had been look alikes. Both with the same dents, creases and lines in their faces, great ears, the same baggage under their eyes... examples of their intensely aware attitudes while performing as well as an imprint of years lived. Both in their '70s, loved by their public... Dempsey shakes hands constantly with everyone as he would with a pal...the Duke embraced his admirers with love...both vintage New Yorkers, equally at home on the subway or in a limousine... since his retirement in '31, Dempsey has been a legend, his profession being Jack Dempsey...he is not unlike a composer who, having written a number of great symphonies by the age of thirty-five, spends the rest of his life conducting them.

253

2-22-'70
LeRoy Neiman
N.Y.

Madison Square Garden
May 16, '67

Carlos Monzon
Argentina
Monte Car

Ellington, on the other hand, created musical works anew all his life, and had been a fighter in the fields of music and race...in the 20s, during the Dempsey era, he played in white-only night clubs... Jack has overcome numerous sociological misunderstandings by virtue of his great fights and warm personality...the Duke's popularity, like the Manassa Mauler's today, was equal with blacks and whites alike.

Fighters Nino Benvenuti and Carlos Monzon carry the same ledges over their eyes...the same scar tissue that always interrupts the growth of the eyebrow...the same type of dents in their noses... the same slow speech style caused by being punched in the throat...a Rorschach ink-blot test, with a line or two here and there, will bring out the personalities of two such veteran fighters without losing their similarities.

Nino Benvenuti
Italy
-7-'71

255

Rocky

Despite their opposite life styles, Rocky Graziano
and Leonard Bernstein are the epitome of New
York's east side — with the same tired eyes, the
same mussed-up look — the pure urban look.
While Bernstein was receiving his degree from Harvard
Graziano was graduating from reform school.

Lenny

In 1942, while Bernstein was a conductor under Koussevitsky, at Berkshire, Rocky was doing time in an army guardhouse; when one ascended the podium of the New York Philharmonic, the other ascended the throne of the middleweight championship.

Hands

The right arm of Leonard Bernstein is more swollen and powerful than his left, like a tennis player's racquet arm...and his right wrist is more developed, like a surgeon's ...reflecting the energy with which he wields his baton...where Bernstein is a twist-of-the-wrist man, Leopold Stokowski conducts with hands of great delicacy, making his demands with the gesture of sensitive fingers...graceful hands are not exclusive with violinists or pianists...the hands have a language of their own...the conductor, the chess master, the gambler placing his bet—the movement of the hand expresses the same forcefulness....True to popular belief, the cardsharp does wind up with the touch...even obese gambling men have the classic tapering fingers...the Vegas look.

1960

Fischer – Spassky   Bobby and Boris   Reykjavick, Iceland   July 27, 73

LeRoy Neiman

LeRoy Neiman

Herbie   Boom Docks   17th St at 10th ave   New York   Aug 15, '71

Free Angela

Leopold
Stokowski
Rehearsal American
Symphony 2-1-'68

necktie loosend

Shouting, waving
his arms,
all the moves a
showman can make
in two hours

LeRoy Neiman

Leonard Bernstein

rolls up sleeves
sings

Jumps—
bounds

A series
of gymnastics

LeRoy Neiman 3-8-67

March 8, '67
Leonard Bernstein
LeRoy Neiman

Rehearsal
N.Y. Phil. Orch.

Eyes

Senator
Ted Kennedy
Atlanta
5-9-'69
LeRoy Neiman

When I drew Ted Kennedy for the first time, in May of 1969, I began by indicating the eyes, as I generally do when sketching the head …I found myself describing the eyes of Bobby.…it could have been any of the Kennedy brothers… later, adding the hair, weight, distributions of expression, it became Ted…I never drew Jack in his lifetime, but did Bobby many times… the Kennedys seem to fill out late, look their most formidable as they approach 40…at the age of 43, Bobby had just reached his permanent Kennedy look.…Some men's eyes show everything they've seen … others show everything they've done…the jockey sees the whole track without moving his head… from his empirical position the maître d' surveys his dining-room domain with lethal eye control… yet the waiter never seems to see you when you try to catch his eye.

"What I resent is that people distort my record and distort what is the truth in connection with this. I demean praise it to just and ... where it is up to..."

"All this Federal gun controls says nation does is keep firearms from people too young, too criminal and the demented... with all the violence and murder in this United States people... they will oppose that... guns..."

"If it is something right now we can't wait to get at."

"Violence won't get us a better society."

"It is a myth at the poor and unemployed do not want to work."

"Human beings need a purpose. We can achieve that purpose if we develop a system where there are jobs able to work for all who are able to work and adequate assistance provided in a dignified way for those who are unable to work." I think that there's a difference between... external aggression and internal aggression.

"We must keep Israel secure against outside aggression."

"We can keep this country moving." "We can do better."

"I have never said, 'You've never had it so good.'"

"I was chief law-enforcement officer of the U.S. for 3½ years. This nation must have law and order."

"All you California people who farm or are in produce should vote for me. Think of all the fruit that is eaten by my family."

"I am not asking favors. I'm not asking your support on the basis that you were friendly to a relative of mine eight years ago..."

"Under no circumstances will I accept running for Vice-president..."

"It is unacceptable that American boys are dying while South Vietnamese boys can buy their way out of the draft."

"My fate is in your hands, but it is less important what happens to me as to what happens to the cause I have tried to present."

RFK

leRoy Neiman '68

DOMAINES DU CHATEAU DE BEAUNE

VINTAGE 195_

CORTON-CHARLEMAGNE

APPELLATION CORTON-CHARLEMAGNE CONTROLÉE

Mise de Maison Bouchard Père & Fils, Négociants au Château, Beaune (Côte d'Or)
PRODUCE OF FRANCE   WHITE BURGUNDY WINE
ALCOHOL 13% BY VOLUME   CONTENTS ½ PINT 8 FL. OZ.
PRODUCED AND BOTTLED BY : BOUCHARD PÈRE & FILS, BEAUNE

Menu
TAILLEVENT
Soufflé au Fromage
Gratin de langouste
Côte de Bœuf grillé

Taillevent
15 R. Lamennais
Paris
LeRoy Neiman

Pete
Maravich
3-19-'70

Willis
Reed
National
Anthem
'73

BERLA
13

Wilt
May 5 '70
M.S.G. N.Y.
LeRoy Neiman

ALCINDOR

Jabbar
march 18 '70
Mad. Square Garden

Rod Laver
M. S.G. N.Y.
May 17 '68
LeRoy Neiman

THOMAS
33

National
ANTHEM SUPER BOWL
Jan 16 '72
LeRoy Neiman
New Orleans

Duane
Thomas

Bill Russell
Mad. Sq. Garden
2-3 '68
LeRoy Neiman

Hyun Kim
Seouil, Korea
126½ 115 fights
New foreign boxer
always has vacination

Dec. 4 '72
Mad. Sq. Gar.

L.A. forum. '73

Intensive Care

The corner in boxing is a kind of field first-aid station—and pulpit ...aside from all his ministrations, and even as he renders this tender aid, the corner man is raising holy hell with his fighter...advising, scolding, lecturing, encouraging, sewing, mending, even sponge-bathing him...the familiar ceremony of yanking out the trunks and sloshing water all over the ringsiders... on major television fights, the custodians of the corner are not unaware of the camera's eye ...they are performing for a nation-wide audience.

march 8 '71
Ali-Frazier
mad. Sq. Garden

LeRoy Neiman

march 24 69
Quarry
Mathis

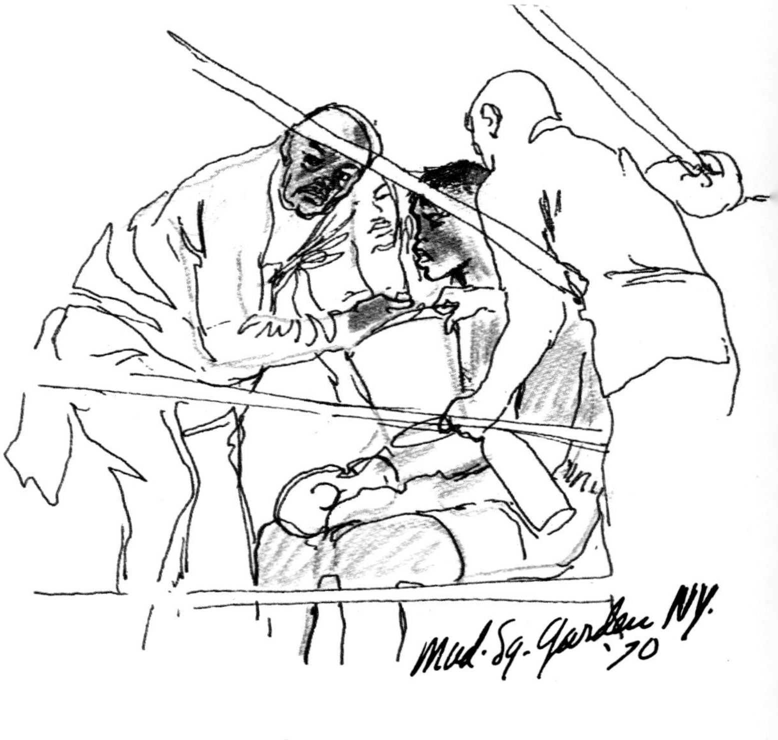

Mad.Sq.Garden NY.
'70

Al Braverman

Boston Gardens '65

Spectrum Philadelphia '70

The classic corner-man pail carrier in the old days was assigned by the manager to stay with the fighter at all times. He made his charge go to bed early so he wouldn't be out nites "lookin' for a little happiness."

A bed sitter, old and broke, he had no temptations challenging him — he was lonely and wanted company — so he insisted fighter be monastic too

March 4 '66

Wembley London

Emile Griffith
V.S.
McAloon
Mad. Sq. Garden
Dec 10, 71

Pamplona

Fiesta de San Fermin, Spain's Woodstock, is an annual young people's revel...it takes youth to run in front of the bulls...to run with the bulls is to run for your life ...all the blurred figures standing in doorways, or leaning from balconies, give the impression that they are blocking your escape in case you seek shelter...horns magnify up close and become the only thing in your vision.

Not to run with the bulls is to leave Pamplona with an incomplete experience....Then we enter the arena to see the fights...to see *el toro* burst into the glaring light of day... for his 15 minutes of gore and glory.

Into the Plaza de Toros

Runners
Red Kerchiefs

Dry Red blood spots on sand

Down final ramp into the tunnel

LeRoy Neiman '73

¡ Una Tarde de Toros !

Salida del Toro
Magnifica entrada

Manolo Martin
Curro Giron
Andres Vazquez

ole

ole   ole

Toreo de capa
o Lances

Frank Sinatra, New York, 1967

BIOGRAPHY

Born in St. Paul, Minnesota—June 8, 1927
Studied at St. Paul Art Center—1946
Studied at School of the Art Institute of Chicago—1946-1950
Member of Faculty, School of the Art Institute of Chicago—1950-1960
Included in "New Talent in America for 1956," published in February 1956 in *Art in
       America*, Cannondale, Connecticut
Painting Instructor, Summer School of Painting, Saugatuck, Michigan—1957, 1958, 1963
Painting Instructor, Arts and Crafts, Inc., Winston-Salem, North Carolina—1963
Instructor, drawing and painting, Atlanta Youth Council—1968, 1969
Listed in *The Art Collector's Almanac*—1965
         Who's Who in American Art—1966-1973
         Who's Who in the East—1970-1975

ONE-MAN EXHIBITIONS

750 Gallery, Chicago—1953
Lincoln College, Lincoln, Illinois—1953
Todes Gallery, Chicago—1957
Chicago Public Library—1958
Oehlschlaeger Gallery, Chicago—1959, 1969
Oehlschlaeger Gallery, Sarasota, Florida—1962
O'Hana Gallery, London—1962
Galerie O. Bosc, Paris—1962
Hammer Gallery, New York—1963, 1965, 1967, 1968, 1970, 1972
Astor Tower Gallery, Chicago—1965
Richelle Gallery, St. Louis—1966
Huntington-Hartford Gallery of Modern Art, New York—1967
Heath Gallery, Atlanta—1969
Abbey Theater, Dublin—1970
Far Gallery, New York—1971
Museo de Bellas Artes, Caracas, Venezuela—1972
Indianapolis Museum of Art, Indianapolis—1972
Circle Galleries, New York, Dallas, Chicago, Los Angeles, San Francisco—1973
Brentano's, Boston, Beverly Hills, New York—1973
Cadaques, Spain—1973
Palm Beach Gallery, Palm Beach, Florida—1973
The Saratoga Gallery, Saratoga, New York—1973
University of Illinois, Urbana, Illinois—1973
University of Texas, El Paso—1973
Tobu Gallery, Tokyo, 1974

With Mae West in New York, 1970

Backstage at the Lido, Paris, 1961

Espace Cardin, Paris — 1974
Springfield Museum of Art, Springfield, Massachusetts — 1974
Gallery Hawaii, Honolulu — 1974

GROUP SHOWS

Carnegie International Exhibition, oil painting, Pittsburgh — 1955
Corcoran American Exhibition, oil painting, Washington, D.C. — 1957
American Exhibition, oil painting, sculpture, Chicago — 1957, 1960
Chicago Artists and Vicinity Show — 1954–1960
St. Paul and Minneapolis Twin-City Show — 1952–1954
Collectors' Show, Walker Art Center, Minneapolis — 1957
Musée des Beaux-Arts, Arras, France — 1958
Museum of Fine Arts, Rouen, France — 1958
Toledo Museum — 1957
Philadelphia Art Alliance — 1958
Werbe Gallery, Detroit — 1958, 1959
Traveling Exhibition, USIS, Holland, France, Germany — 1957 to 1959
Society of Contemporary American Art Exhibition, Chicago — 1958, 1959, 1960
Ringling Museum American Art Exhibition, Sarasota, Florida — 1959
Des Moines Art Center — 1960
Butler Institute of American Art, Youngstown, Ohio — 1960
Salon d'Art Moderne, Paris — 1961
Galerie Cécile de Terssac, Cannes, France — 1962
Sir Francis Peak Gallery, Nassau, Bahamas — 1962
Galerie 18, Paris — 1963
Shore Gallery, Boston — 1963
John Heron Museum of Art, Indianapolis — 1964
Galleria Fiorentina d'Arte, Florence — 1964
Houston Art Gallery, Houston, Texas — 1967, 1974
Harmon Gallery, Naples, Florida — 1968
Minnesota Museum of Art, St. Paul — 1969
National Portrait Gallery, The Smithsonian Institution, Washington, D.C. — 1970
Forsyth Gallery, St. Louis — 1970
Rotunda della Besana, Milan — 1971
Royal College of Art, London — 1971
Print International, Basel — 1971, 1972, 1973
Circle Galleries, New York, Dallas, Chicago, Los Angeles, San Francisco — 1972
Koninklijk Museum voor Schone Kunsten, Antwerp — 1972
Gemeentemuseum, Arnham, The Netherlands — 1972
Kunstverein München, Munich — 1972
Musée des Arts Décoratifs, Lausanne, Switzerland — 1972

Janet Neiman, Felicie Schumsky, Linda Moreno, 1971

Central Museum of Art, Tokyo — 1973
Umeda Kindai Museum, Osaka — 1973
Lowe Museum, University of Miami, Coral Gables, Florida — 1974
Hermitage Museum, Leningrad — 1974
Los Angeles Municipal Museum, Los Angeles — 1974
FKH Gallery, New York — 1974

AWARDS

1st Prize, Oil Painting, Twin-City Show — 1953
2nd Prize, Oil Painting, Minnesota State Show — 1954
Clark Memorial Prize, Oil Painting, Chicago Show — 1957
Hamilton and Graham Cash Prize, Ball State Teachers Show — 1958
Municipal Art Award, Oil Painting, Chicago Show — 1958
Purchase Prize, Oil Painting, Mississippi Valley Show — 1959
Gold Medal, Salon d'Art Moderne, Paris — 1961

PUBLIC MURALS

Continental Hotel, Chicago — 1963
Mercantile National Bank, Hammond, Indiana — 1966
Swedish Lloyd Ship, S.S. Patricia, Stockholm — 1966
Playboy Resort Hotel, Lake Geneva, Wisconsin — 1967
Playboy Resort Hotel, Great Gorge, New Jersey — 1971

MUSEUM AND PUBLIC COLLECTIONS

Hermitage Museum, Leningrad
Indianapolis Museum of Art
Minneapolis Institute of Arts
Museo de Bellas Artes, Caracas, Venezuela
Illinois State Museum, Springfield, Illinois
Joslyn Museum, Omaha, Nebraska
Wodham College, Oxford, England
National Museum of Sport in Art, New York City
Harding Museum, Chicago
Hayward Museum, Hayward, California
University of Texas
University of Illinois
Springfield Museum of Art, Springfield, Massachusetts
Mobile Art Gallery and Museum, Mobile, Alabama

Publisher's Note: For those readers and researchers who wish further references on the artist, the publisher provides this listing of articles and other materials.

"Key Club, Casino and Race Track Are Painted by LeRoy Neiman," Frank Getlein, *Milwaukee Journal*, October 27, 1957.
"Down at Neiman's Bar and Grill," Frank Getlein, *The New Republic*, November 11, 1957.
"Chicagoan's Bar Baroque," Meyer Levin, *Chicago American*, December 8, 1957.
"Painter of the Urban Scene," *Playboy*, April 1958, pp. 49—51.
"Painting His Way into Nation's Restaurants," Dorothy Walker, *San Francisco News*, July 26, 1958.
"LeRoy Neiman's Passion for the Posh," *San Francisco Examiner*, August 1, 1958.
"Show Young Artist's Bold Work," Barnard K. Leiter, *Chicago Daily News*, October 12, 1959.
"There is Nothing Still about the Life This Artist Paints," Mervin Block, *Chicago American*, November 3, 1959.
"El Pintor Americano Neiman viene a captar escenas tipicas Madrileñas," Sanchez Cobos, *Madrid*, April 29, 1960.
"LeRoy Neiman—An Exuberant Painter," William Caxton, Jr., *American Artist*, April 1961.
"He'll Paint Bardot—Sans Towel," Will Jones, *Minneapòlis Sun Tribune*, April 10, 1961.
"Gambling on Canvas," Peterborough, London Day by Day, *The Daily Telegraph*, February 22, 1962.
"Artist Neiman Dances as the Cash Rolls In," Roger Beardwood, In London Last Night, *Evening Standard*, March 9, 1962.
"All Bedlam Broke Loose at O'Hana Gallery Last Thursday Evening," Arts and Entertainment, C. R. Cammell, *New Daily*, London, March 14, 1962.
"Expressionism on the American Scene," *Topic Magazine*, London, March 17, 1962.
"LeRoy Neiman at O'Hana Gallery," Michael Shepherd, *Arts Review*, London, March 1962.
"Peripatetic Portrait Painter," Carol Pinsky, *Select Magazine*, March 1962.
"Les Expositions du Peintre Americain LeRoy Neiman," André Weber, *Juvenal*, Paris, November 30, 1962.
"LeRoy Neiman—Un Homme Solide," Honoré Bostel, *Galerie O. Bosc Catalogue*, Paris, November 1962.
"LeRoy Neiman's New Canvases," Paris Galleries, *New York Herald Tribune* (Paris), December 1, 1962.
"LeRoy Neiman-Hammer," October 8-19, *Art News*, October 1963.
"Printmaker and Painter—Deen Meeker and LeRoy Neiman," Frank Getlein, *New Republic*, November 30, 1963.
"Artist LeRoy Neiman," Tony Weitzel, *Chicago Daily News*, January 14, 1965.
"American's View of Paris Smart Set," Harold Haydon, *Chicago Sun Times*, February 7, 1965.
"High Life," Edward Barry, art editor, *Chicago Tribune*, Febuary 21, 1965.
"Thriving in World of Chaos," Phyllis Battelle, *New York Journal American*, July 24, 1965.
"Artist Leroy Neiman Unveils Himself at Bank," Gerald J. Bayles, *Hammond Times*, Hammond, Indiana, February 18, 1966.
"Putting Clubland in the Picture," Franklyn Wood, *Daily Sketch*, London, June 27, 1966.
"Famous Faces by Playboy Artist," *London Life*, London, July 2, 1966.
"A Bartender's Best Friend," *Miami Beach Sun*, April 4, 1967.
"Jill St. John," *Miami Herald Sunday Magazine*, May 14, 1967.
"Leonard Bernstein-LeRoy Neiman," *Arts Magazine*, September-October 1967.
"An Original," Larry Merchant, *New York Post*, December 5, 1967.
"Girl Watching in Moscow," Anthony C. Collins, *New York Post*, April 1, 1968.
"Giving the World the Brush," *New York Sunday News*, April 21, 1968.
"Too Much Chaos?" Phyllis Battelle, *Record American*, Boston, July 29, 1968.
"Artist Poses Famous People," Ann Carter, art editor, *Atlanta Journal*, September 6, 1968.
"Pigskin Picasso," Maury Allen, *New York Post*, November 5, 1968.
"Portrait in Jet," Sidney Fields, Only Human, *New York Daily News*, December 26, 1968.
"Neiman Sketches the Sport of His Times," Stan Isaacs, *Newsday*, September 1968.
"An Artist's Impression of Jets," Mickey Herskowitz, *Houston Post*, November 11, 1968.
"Jets Immortalized in Vivid Colors," Barney Nagler, *Morning Telegraph*, January 4, 1969.
"LeRoy Neiman's Atlantans," *Atlanta Magazine*, May 1969.
"Neiman Sees Prosperity in Title Bout," Dave Brady, *Washington Post*, June 22, 1969.
"Local Boy Paints Good," Oliver Town, *St. Paul Dispatch-Pioneer Press*, December 9, 1969.
"Figure-ing Fighters," Roy McHugh, sports editor, *Pittsburgh Press*, December 16, 1969.
"Oh, How LeRoy Suffers for His Art," Larry Merchant, *Jock Magazine*, February 1970.
"LeRoy Neiman Sketches Bunny of the Year," *VIP Magazine*, Spring 1970.

"LeRoy Neiman, World Series Artist," Pat Harmon, sports editor, *Pittsburgh Courier*, October 1970.

"LeRoy Neiman—The Rembrandt of the Ring," *Boxing Illustrated*, March 1971.

"En el Museo de Bellas Artes Exponer Briceno y Neiman," *La Verdad*, Caracas, April 23, 1972.

"Reportajes en Dibujos sobre Canonero en el Museo de Bellas Artes de Caracas," *El Nacional*, Caracas, April 28, 1972.

"Dibujos al Minuto y Esculturas Estaticas," *El Nacional*, Caracas, May 4, 1972.

"Neiman—Sports Artist-in-Residence," Nick Seitz, *Christian Science Monitor*, May 2, 1972.

"Neiman Fits Avant-garde Artist Role," *Asbury Park Sunday Press*, September 2, 1972.

"LeRoy Neiman—A Sense of Humor in His Work," Dick Olmstead, Press Box, *Tribune Chronicle*, Warren, Ohio, September 27, 1972.

"Artist LeRoy Neiman—From Poverty to Playboy," *Indianapolis News*, November 23, 1972.

"Introducing LeRoy Neiman," Carl J. Weinhardt, Director, Indianapolis Museum of Art, Catalog of XX Olympiad, November 22, 1972.

"Making the Scene—Marigold Gardens and the Strip Joints to Realms of the Rich. Neiman's Reflections of Chicago," *Chicago Sunday Sun Times*, December 3, 1972.

"LeRoy Neiman Prefers to Paint Real People," Patricia Shelton, Everyday, *Chicago Daily News*, December 8, 1972.

"LeRoy Neiman Sketches the Girls of Indianapolis," Susan Lennis, *Indianapolis Star Magazine*, December 24, 1972.

"LeRoy Neiman: He Brushes Off Success," Alan Eskew, *Dallas Times Herald*, February 9, 1973.

"Portrait of the Artist as Bon Vivant," Paul-Hayden Parker, *Mainliner Magazine*, United Air Lines, April 1973.

"Documentary Sketches—Expressions of Our Times," Al Bine, *Los Angeles Herald-Examiner*, June 24, 1973.

The following is a list of paintings used in the Sketchbook section of the book.

Finish at Ascot, 1973   pages 118–119
oil, 36″ x 48″
Collection of the artist

Newmarket Heath, 1964   pages 124–125
mixed media, 19″ x 24″
Collection of the artist

Start at Indy, 1962   page 132
oil, 50″ x 40″
Collection of Mrs. Anton Hulman, Jr.,
Terre Haute, Indiana

Pits at Can-Am Race, 1970   page 133
oil, 48″ x 36″
From the Playboy Collection

The Stag's Head, 1961   pages 136–137
mixed media, 22″ x 30″
Collection of the artist

Via Veneto, 1967   pages 140–141
mixed media, 22″ x 30″
Collection of the artist

Before the Decision, 1971   pages 150–151
mixed media, 22″ x 30″
Collection of the artist

Harlequin, 1971   page 156
oil, 72″ x 48″
Collection of the Honorable and Mrs.
Anthony G. DiFalco, New York City

De Gaulle, 1962   page 164
Napoleon, 1962
both oil on paper, 40″ x 30″
Collection of Mr. Harrison Eiteljorg,
Indianapolis, Indiana

Photography Credits

page 8 — photo by Alexas Urba
pages 15, 81, 102 — photos by Neil Leifer
page 94, back of jacket — photos by Rick Cluthe
pages 100, 101 — photos by Fred Kaplan
page 101 — photo by Takashi Makita
page 280 — photo by Dan Jacino

Printed in Italy by Arnoldo Mondadori Editore - Verona